T0146416

Walking
WITH
God

Lessons on Intimacy which I have
learnt along the Journey

MODUPE SANUSI

authorHOUSE®

AuthorHouse™ UK
1663 Liberty Drive
Bloomington, IN 47403 USA
www.authorhouse.co.uk
Phone: 0800.197.4150

Scripture quotations marked KJV are from the Holy Bible, King James Version
(Authorized Version). First published in 1611. Quoted from the KJV Classic
Reference Bible, Copyright © 1983 by The Zondervan Corporation.

Published by AuthorHouse 03/08/2019

ISBN: 978-1-5246-7779-4 (sc)
ISBN: 978-1-5246-7780-0 (hc)
ISBN: 978-1-5246-7778-7 (e)

Print information available on the last page.

This book is printed on acid-free paper.

Contents

Growth

Virtue is not an end in itself. Virtue is not the most important thing we are seeking to possess on this journey towards Christ. This is where the majority of ethicists and philosophers have gone wrong. Virtue and justice is a means to an end and the end is God, or more namely an intimacy shared with God. God is who we are looking to enjoin ourselves to and God is He who we are looking to become unmistakably identical to. We want to know God like Moses knew Him. We want to be so similar, so completely identical to Him, that like the Lord Jesus Christ we may unashamedly affirm "I and my Father are One [Jn 10:30]." We need to know how we might achieve this, and whilst the first step in this journey is to cling unto a faith in the Lord Jesus Christ, there are additional steps – in terms of our moral disposition – which must be exercised daily in order to improve our communion with God.

In the second epistle of Peter the Apostle exhorted the church to "grow in grace, and in the knowledge of our Lord and Saviour Jesus Christ [2 Pet 3:18]." He also exhorted the church to grow in faith, virtue, knowledge, temperance, patience, godliness, brotherly kindness and charity. He told them: "for if these things be in you, and abound, they make you that ye shall neither be barren nor unfruitful in the knowledge of our Lord Jesus Christ [2 Pet 1:8]."

This is something the Apostle Paul instructed his disciples too. To Timothy for instance he told him to "follow righteousness, faith, charity, peace with them that call on the Lord out of a pure heart [2 Tim 2:22]." And in another epistle to Timothy the Apostle gave a similar exhortation, instructing him to "follow after righteousness, godliness, faith, love, patience, meekness [1 Tim 6:11]." These are some of the virtues we will be examining over the course of this text. They are clearly important because Timothy was already a fervent believer who had gained a good reputation in the faith. Before Timothy meet Paul and was taken under his arm he was already "well reported of by the brethren that were at Lystra and Iconium [Acts 16:2]." Timothy was in the faith of Jesus Christ before he meet Paul and he was already known for his good character by those who maintained fellowship with him. Paul discipled him further and they became formidably close over the course of their respective lives. Timothy was a very trustworthy man and Paul could not find many comparable to him. Subsequently he was safely entrusted with large responsibilities and jobs to complete in overseeing some of the churches which were established by his spiritual father.

In the epistle to the Philippians Paul said this of Timothy. "But I trust in the Lord Jesus to send Timotheus shortly unto you, that I also maybe of good comfort, when I know your state [Phi 2:19]." Paul was in prison when he wrote and sent this epistle. He had planned to send Timothy to the church at Philippi to help oversee their ongoing progress. Paul knew a lot of men in the faith and he had worked tirelessly to disciple many growing believers. But out of a large pot of believers he decided to choose only Timothy. Here is why: "For I have no man likeminded, who will naturally care for your state. For all seek their own, not the things which are Jesus Christ's [Phi 2:20-21]." Timothy was completely sold out to serve Jesus Christ. He did not do so from a place of selfish ambition or vainglory, he did not do so as a means to an end, to receive some other baser good such as money or esteem from men, but he did so because he was intimate with Christ and loved him.

But despite all of these good remarks Paul still exhorted the disciple to grow in righteousness and virtue.

We should never believe we have reached perfection and that there is no more room to continue growing. Paul acknowledged this when he conceded to the Philippians that he had not yet attained perfection but he continued to press on towards the mark for the prize of the high calling of God in Christ Jesus [Phi 3:13-14]. The truth is that there is always space to grow. We can always become wiser, stronger, kinder, more meek, more patient and gentle. We should never say we have fulfilled all of our potential with regards to spiritual growth. If we do so then we will never leave space for future growth. If I already think I am wise or if I already think I have learnt all knowledge then I will not desire growth in these areas. But if I like to learn and I understand that there is still a lot more to learn then I will be incentivised to pursue more knowledge. It is wise therefore to always maintain a space for spiritual growth.

It is good to continue learning. "A wise man will hear, and will increase learning; and a man of understanding shall attain unto wise counsels [Pro 1:5]." Nobody knows everything. For we see in part, know in part and prophecy in part. The same thing most obviously applies to our knowledge of God. Who among us can say we know everything about God? Everyday we should strive to learn something new about God. There is still much more to discover about God.

If there is one thing I love about the spiritual life is that we are constantly evolving. Constantly discovering layers of God which lie dormant within. Constantly labouring until Christ is perfectly and wholly formed within. Because he is so vast and so enthusiastic about the opportunity of teaching us more of his righteous ways, he will often give us much more revelation than we initially expected or desired. This is why Paul says He is able to do exceedingly and more abundantly than we can think or desire [Eph 3:20]. But never must we say that we have learnt everything which ought to be ascertained. This will only stifle any spiritual growth.

If we are still alive on this earth then it must mean that there is still something for us to do which God wants us to achieve before we die. If you remain alive on the earth and you have yet to be taken up by God then it simply means that you have not yet fulfilled your purpose and that there is still more growth and learning which must be undergone before you stand before the Lord in judgement. When Jesus Christ was on the cross he cried "it is finished [Jn 19:30]." And when he prayed to the Father shortly before he was betrayed by Judas and taken into imprisonment he proclaimed "I have finished the work which thou gavest me to do [Jn 17:4]." Because Jesus had accomplished the work which God had sent him into the world to do, there remained no more reason for him to stay upon the earth. The same applied to Enoch, Elijah and John the Baptist. They finished the work which God had ordained for them to do and so he took them into the comfort and peace of his heavenly chambers.

There were a number of times when plots were made against Jesus to take his life. But we often heard of how "no man laid hands on him because his hour was not yet come [Jn 7:30]." There is a similar story of two witnesses whom will arise in the last days prophesying for 1260 days. They are sealed by God and will withstand all persecution plotted against them until they have finished their God ordained testimony. They will only be killed once they have finished their testimony.

God will not let us die until we achieve what he has purposed for us to fulfil. God wants us to bear fruit and to bear fruit in abundance. Without the fruit of the Spirit we cannot enter into heaven. So God will often wait patiently until we begin producing the fruit of righteousness which he so desperately desires. "Behold the husbandman waiteth for the precious fruit of the earth and hath long patience for it, until he receive the early and latter rain [Jas 5:7]." When we begin producing the fruit of the Spirit and fulfil our specific mandate upon the earth, God will not tarry in leaving us here. But instead he will send forth his sickle to reap the well-anticipated fruit of the earth. This is a principle which is alluded to in the gospel of Mark. In the gospel of Mark we are told by Jesus: "but when fruit is brought forth, immediately he putteth in the sickle, because the harvest is come [Mk 4:29]."

God will not take us until the fruit of the Spirit is flourishing in our life! This of course does not apply to everybody; for we will not all bear good fruit. Some trees bear no fruit and some trees bear bad fruit. But every tree which God waters will one day bear good fruit: and when the harvest has come, with its fruit in abundance, he will surely not tarry before sending his angels to thrust his sickle into the earth.

This clearly shows us that we must continue to grow until God takes us. If we are alive today then it must mean God wants us to still develop our growth. And if we refuse to grow into the likeness of his Son then we will face severe repercussions. There is therefore ample space and grace for us to continue learning.

But let us not be like those who are "ever learning, and never able to come to the knowledge of the truth [2 Tim 3:7]." For there is a big difference between those who learn for mere theological information and those who learn the things of God because they want to apply his word and thereby grow into his likeness. Let us be doers of the word and let us immediately put into practise everything we learn from God on a daily basis.

Everybody must undergo growth in the kingdom of God. Even Jesus had to, and in his youth he increased in wisdom and stature, and in favour with God and man [Lk 2:52]. Jesus was able to achieve this because he was continually learning from God and applying what he had learnt from Him on a practical basis. There are some deeper things God cannot teach us until we have learnt to apply what he has already told us before. God can only teach us deeper things when we have first learnt to apply the basic foundations. This is how all learning works. As an English Teacher I cannot teach you how to write a story if you have not first learnt how to write a sentence. And as a Mathematics Teacher I cannot teach you about algebra if you have not first learnt about the application of addition and subtraction. The same principle applies to the things of God. He cannot teach you about love if you have not yet learnt how to apply faith. He cannot teach you about prayer if you have not yet learnt about forgiveness. And he cannot teach you about heavenly secrets from above if we have not yet learnt about obedience. This is why it is so crucial for us to hearken unto every word of the Lord; so that we might progress rather than stagnate, so that we might move forward rather than backwards.

The Kingdom of God is about growth. Jesus Christ says that the Kingdom of God is like a mustard seed which is the least of all seeds but later grows into the greatest of trees [Matt 13:31-32]. When we are in the kingdom of God we will not be the same person we were yesterday but we ought to progress everyday as God teaches us something new each day. He is a God who loves you and who desires to impart new revelation into you each new hour. When we hearken unto these new revelations, and his continual counsel, then we are compelled to continually grow.

We do not need to wait a long time before we flourish into the fruitful trees which God seeks to glorify in the midst of men. We must learn how to abide in him so that he might abide in us. Jesus was 30 years old when he began his ministry and only needed to work for around three years before accomplishing his own assignment. He was able to achieve this because he learnt quickly and immediately applied everything which he was taught. This is such an important principle which we cannot underestimate. I can remember when I was learning how to play a trumpet. I had never learnt how to play a wind-pipe instrument before and I found it tremendously difficult to blow it and make the right sound. In the first two lessons, I had still not learnt how to blow it properly. The teacher was teaching me the particular technique I had to apply with my lips, chin and tongue but I could not learn anything else; any notes, any songs, any pitches, until I had first learnt the most basic requirement. The same thing holds true in the Kingdom of God. We cannot accomplish greater assignments when we have not yet accomplished the smaller and more foundational ones.

The same applies to us believers when we do not learn the most basic requirements for our walk with God. If I do not know how to love, walk in humility, and forgiveness, then there is no way God will advance me into deeper things. This is a major problem which has stifled much spiritual progress within the body of Christ. Intellectual knowledge may increase but experiential knowledge stagnates or even diminishes and there is no ostensible evidence of the power of God. All of this happens because of our inability to apply the word of God: because many of us believers are hearers of the words but not doers. Jesus Christ was rich in experiential knowledge of God, as well as intellectual knowledge. This is because he learnt the word of God daily and he also applied it into his life regularly. This is why he did not need to stay on the earth for too long. Jesus understood that effectiveness is better than longevity. In other words it is better that we leave a formidable and exceptional legacy even if we live for a short period of time than if we live for a long time and yet make little or no far-reaching improvement before we die.

You will be surprised how far God can take you in the space of one year if you but only obey his word and daily seek to learn his ways. Look at the example of Isaac, the son of Abraham who "sowed in the land of the Philistines and received in the same year an hundredfold [Gen 26:12]." The great thing about this story is that Isaac managed to do this whilst the world was facing a famine. The same is surely promised to us when we continually learn and adhere to the principles of the kingdom of God.

"And the child grew, and waxed strong in spirit, filled with wisdom: and the grace of God was upon him. [Lk 2:40]"

"And Jesus increased in wisdom and stature, and in favour with God and man. [Lk 2:52]"

"And the child Samuel grew on, and was in favour both with the Lord, and also with men. [1 Sam 2:26]"

"And Samuel grew, and the Lord was with him, and did let none of his words fall to the ground. [1 Sam 3:19]"

PRACTICAL STEPS FOR GROWTH

- Read the word of God every day. Read it and obey it. Look for ways to make the word of God practical in your life. Do not strive for head knowledge but always look for opportunities to profit from the word of God in every area of your life.
- Pray in the Spirit for at least one hour each day.
- Stay in fellowship with other like-minded believers who are also interested in growth. Find a prayer partner who will stir you to increase your spiritual growth.
- Find a mentor who you can become accountable to. If you find this difficult then pray to God that he will find you somebody to help mentor you.
- Strive to improve every day. You should be a better, more productive person than you were yesterday.
- Evaluate your life daily in comparison to the Lord Jesus. Whilst it is helpful to compare yourself to other believers who are doing exploits for the Kingdom it will always be better and more useful to ultimately compare yourself to the works which Jesus did.
- Document your plans and objectives. Are they being meet? Are you accomplishing less or more than what you set out to achieve? Speak to God to discover which areas of growth He wants you to focus on. He will provide grace for you to become better. But daily evaluate your progress.

Walking with God

In the book of Genesis we are given a small glimpse into the life of a holy man who walked with God. His name was Enoch. "And Enoch lived sixty and five years, and begat Methuselah. And Enoch walked with God after he begat Methuselah three hundred years, and begat sons and daughters. [Gen 5:21-22]."

Enoch did not always walk with God. But when he was 65 years old he made the choice to consecrate his whole life unto God. He decided to offer up his body as a living sacrifice unto the Lord. He choose to dedicate everything which he said or did unto the name and cause of the Lord. He genuinely wanted to please God and know him more intimately. He subsequently walked with God for 300 years. He did not walk with God from the day of his birth or from his adolescence but he made the decision to do so at the age of 65.

We too can make the decision to walk with God today. We should never make the mistake of saying we will give our lives to the Lord when we are older, sometime next year or when we have finally overcome the familiar lusts of adolescence. We should not make this mistake because tomorrow is not guaranteed to anybody. We ought to remember that "man is like to vanity: his days are as a shadow that passeth away [Psa 144:4]." Our lives are very short and the sooner we decide to give our all unto the Lord then the more we will be able to achieve for Him during this brief sojourn called life. It does not matter whether we are old or whether we are young. We are alive and as long as there is life there is still hope for change. Enoch made this decision and chose to walk with God for 300 years. He made his decision when he was comparatively old. A similar story is recounted in the life of Abraham who started walking with the LORD when he was seventy five. Whereas our Lord

Jesus made the decision to walk with the LORD from a very young age. I believe the younger we give our lives unto God the better.

Nevertheless during the time Enoch walked with God, God revealed to him many things. God taught him something new every day. Enoch was surrounded by the peace and wisdom of God during every step he took. Enoch spent most of his time with God alone. For lovers love to be alone. They enjoyed communing with one another and they subsequently became very familiar with one another. We can say they became good friends.

"And all the days of Enoch were three hundred sixty and five years: And Enoch walked with God: and he was not; for God took him." [Gen 5:23-24]

When you walk with somebody for a long time you will undoubtedly learn a lot about that person. You will not only have intellectual knowledge of that person but you will also gain experiential knowledge of them. Enoch walked with God for 300 years and there was still so much more for him to learn by the time God took him. But God filled him up with a lot of revelation and a lot of heavenly mysteries because Enoch hungered for His truth and he had come to prioritise fellowship with Him above all other things. God is said to be rewarder of those who diligently seek Him [Heb 11:6] and Enoch certainly discovered this principle during his life. Jesus reminds us today: "blessed are those who hunger and thirst for righteousness; for they shall be filled [Matt 5:6]." The same can be said for those who hunger and thirst for companionship with God. The same can be said for those who hunger and thirst for his favour and his anointing.

In the book of Hebrews we are told "by faith Enoch was translated that he should not see death; and was not found, because God had translated him; for before his translation he had this testimony, that he pleased God [Heb 11:5]." One of the encouraging lessons we can take from the story of Enoch is that he pleased God. This passage shows us clearly that it is possible to please God. God is a personal being and he can be either pleased or displeased. Enoch discovered how to please the LORD and he walked with him for the remainder of his life doing so. If Enoch, who is a man, pleased the LORD then we all have the opportunity to please God too.

God is pleased when we walk with Him. But there are some procedures we must take in order to please him so that He might desire to walk with us. God is also pleased when He walks with us. It is God's will that he might walk with all of his people for the remainder of their lives. This was God's plan from the beginning and he still ardently desires communion today. Enoch understood this and he learnt over a period of time what he had to do in order to walk with Him daily.

"Let thy talk be with the wise, and all thy communication in the law of the most High." [Sirach 9:15]

Enoch prioritised fellowship with God over all other people. All other fellowships he shared upon the earth were founded upon his desire to have fellowship with God. If God was not in the midst of any fellowship he entertained upon the earth then he would have certainly ended that friendship abruptly. Every relationship was centred around his desire to walk with God. When he spoke to other people he would only speak about God and he would only share what God had told him to speak. He was holy, for God is holy; so he only spoke about topics which were orientated around the LORD. And he was a man of consistent and continual prayer. He learnt to speak to God as a friend. He did not need to shout or repeat vain repetitions when he spoke to God and he certainly did not scream incantations into the air when he was praying. Although Enoch knew that God's throne was in the heavens he also understood that God was very near unto all those who walk in faith.

Here are some practical lessons we can apply from the life of Enoch. This is what he did and we should follow his example:

- Prioritise fellowship with God above all things. This requires you to spend ample time with him daily. Devote hours alone to spend with God. The first few hours of each day should be spent alone with God. Prayer, worship and reading of the scripture ought to be done first thing in the morning. Learn to wake up earlier to consecrate time unto God.
- Become hungry for God. Maintain this hunger all throughout your life. Strive to be the hungriest person for God in the world.

- Seek to please God in your conduct, character, deeds and words. Remember God is a personal being; a Father whom we can please.
- Establish healthy friendships which are centred upon intimacy with God. Pray to God that he will help you establish these relationships.
- Speak to God throughout the day as you would do with a companion. However respect and revere him. He is Almighty and your life is in his hands.

God has a Personality

Whenever you walk with somebody there are usually one of three things which take place. Either you are talking to the person you are walking with, or you are listening to the person, or both of you are walking in silence, meditating and daydreaming about past or future plans and events. Enoch did all of these as he walked with God. He was either talking to God (in prayer), listening to God, or meditating upon God. Enoch was always thinking about God because he enjoyed His presence. Enoch understood that his thought process could act as a magnet to draw the presence of the LORD. He could not wait to speak to Him and to receive fresh revelation about God's plans for the day.

God did not force Enoch to walk with Himself, but Enoch compelled the Father to walk with him. God responds to principles which he has set forth in his Word and if we adhere to these principles then God has no choice but to respond to us.

One of the most surprising statements we can find in the bible is in the book of Malachi. It is startling because it reveals God's personality in a way we do not typically envisage or discuss. "Was not Esau Jacob's brother? saith the LORD: yet I loved Jacob, and I hated Esau, and laid his mountains and his heritage waste [Mal 1:2-3]." The scripture is clear: God has people whom he loves and people whom he despises. This is revealing because it reveals the fact that God has a clear personality. There are some people God favours and wants to walk with and there are others who, out of the consequences of their own actions and heart, he frowns upon and decides to turn his face from.

Who among us would decide to walk with somebody who they did not enjoy being around? Some of us would not walk with certain people for even one hour. But God decided to walk with Enoch for 300 years. He clearly loved the presence of his friend Enoch. Can many of us honestly say we have walked with God for even one whole day?

Enoch walked with God primarily because he came to understand that the Lord of spirits is a personal being who delights in communion and worship. Enoch could not walk with a piece of wood or a hedge of stone but Enoch could walk with God because He is a living intelligence. When we walk with somebody for a prolonged period of time we learn something new about that person each time. Rarely do we walk with people who do not open up to us and reveal something new to us each day. And rarely will we desire to walk with somebody who is not willing to teach us something new each day. We will not walk with somebody who is not warm, loving and patient. We will not walk with somebody who does not have a sense of humour and who does not have wisdom. And neither will we desire to walk with somebody who does not want to walk with us. We want to walk with people who benefit us and uplift us in some way. God even walks with us because he sees that there is certain benefit for Himself in doing so. Enoch also desired to walk with the LORD because of the benefits he received from doing so. These were not material benefits by any means but they were spiritual ones such as peace, love and joy. He also walked with God because he simply liked the LORD as a person in Himself. He wanted to walk with God because he realised and experienced the great value of maintaining a daily relationship with God.

If we walk with somebody for long enough we will eventually form a strong bond with them. But if somebody no longer finds the friendship valuable he will break the bond and no longer walk with the other person. Some people form friendships because one party will benefit financially from the other party. "For some man is a friend for his own occasion, and will not abide in the day of thy trouble. . . Again, some friend is a companion at the table, and will not continue in the day of thy affliction . . . If thou be brought low, he will be against thee, and will hide himself from thy face [Sirach 6:8,10,12]." However, when there is mutual value in a friendship then it will last for a lifetime.

Enoch never broke his bond with God; he never decided to stop walking with God. This is because God never failed him. God never decided to stop walking with Enoch too. This is because Enoch was faithful and continued to seek after His fellowship. It takes two to walk together. And if God walked with Enoch he must have enjoyed doing so too. God wants to walk with his people because he finds great value in doing so. Otherwise He would have not decided to walk with Enoch for so long; and neither would he have told the prophet Micah to "walk humbly with thy God [Mic 6:8]." One of the reasons why man was created was to worship God. One of the ways in which we can worship God is by harbouring a deep desire to walk with Him continually.

It has always been God's desire to walk with man. Adam was created to walk with God in harmony and in obedience. When he and Eve disobeyed the word of the LORD "they heard the voice of the LORD God walking in the garden in the cool of the day [Gen 3:8]." The garden of Eden (Paradise) is not like the realm we currently inhabit. The realm in the garden of Eden was principally spiritual. And God is not a man but a Spirit. So Adam walked with God not in quite the same way in which a man walks with another physical man but Adam walked with God in the spiritual realm. This is how Enoch walked with God too. And this is how the disciples of Jesus can follow Christ to this very day.

John in the book of Revelation sees those who stood on mount Sion with Jesus Christ, "they which follow the Lamb whithersoever he goeth [Rev 14:4]." When Jesus was living on the earth his disciples could walk with the body of God because Jesus is the fullness of Godhead bodily [Col 2:9]. But men and women of God can still walk with God today despite Jesus ascending into heaven. This is because he has given us his Holy Ghost. Enoch and Adam walked with God despite there being no tangible body to walk with, which indicates that God can walk with us in the spiritual realm. This is what Jesus told his disciples before he ascended into heaven. "Lo, I am with you always, even unto the end of the world [Matt 28:20]." When the scripture speaks of somebody walking with God it is indicating a close proximity between two persons. It is a metaphorical way of indicating intimacy between two individuals.

The Holy Spirit is the breathe and life of God. When we walk with God the Holy Spirit is both upon us and within us. We might not be able to see God's Spirit because it is not discerned by the natural eye. He is invisible but that does not prevent us from feeling his presence from within our own spirit. "The Spirit itself beareth witness with our spirit, that we are the children of God [Rom 8:16]."

In the book of Genesis Moses recounts how "the LORD was with Joseph [Gen 39:2]." God was with Joseph in the realm of the spirit. And in the book of Ezekiel the prophet recounts how the hand of the LORD was upon him [Eze 1:6]. God did not put a physical hand upon Ezekiel. But he placed a spiritual hand upon him, a hand which is not discerned by the flesh but which has much more of a substantive reality than the world which is observed by the natural eye.

"As God hath said, I will dwell in them, and walk in them; and I will be their God, and they shall be my people [2 Cor 6:16]."

There is a spiritual body and there is a physical body. God walks with us with our spiritual body. But God will only decide to walk with us if we do those thing which please him. " [For] can two walk together, except they be agreed? [Amos 3:3]."

Although God wants to walk with us we must first learn how to follow him. Joshua learnt how to walk with Moses because he first followed him. Elisha learnt how to walk with Elijah because he first followed him. The same applies to the disciples of Jesus Christ. "Henceforth I call you not servants: for the servant knoweth not what his lord doeth: but I have called you friends; for all things that I have heard of my Father I have made known unto you [Jn 15:15]."

We follow Jesus when we obey his principles and words by faith. If we obey Jesus then we follow him in the Spirit. God can lead us in the Spirit even if we do not see him. "And Jesus being full of the Holy Ghost returned from Jordan, and was led by the Spirit into the wilderness [Lk 4:1]." We are walking with God when we are being led by the Spirit. But the Spirit will only led us when He sees that we are willing to be led. The Spirit is a person rather than some type of impersonal force. The Spirit we are discussing presently *is* God and we are aware that He is personal. This is why Paul admonished the Ephesians not to grieve the Holy Spirit [Eph 4:30]. God can be grieved by some of the decisions we make and some of the motives we harbour in our heart. If we continue to grieve God then he will decide to stop walking with us [1 Sam 16:14]. So we must therefore choose to do those things which please him so that he might decide to favour us and walk with us. This walk is a two-way relationship and walking with God requires loyalty. But we must acknowledge how when we stop walking with God we are walking with some other type of strange spirit.

If we make the choice to walk with God we must learn those things which please him. Many of us would improve our walk with God if we knew those things which pleased Him and we applied them to our lives daily.

If God can be pleased with us then he can also be displeased with us. Our responsibilities is to discover what pleases him and then to practise it. When we do so we will bear a lot of spiritual fruit.

Walking means that we travel with God. When we walk with God we will follow wherever he leads us to. It is important for us to walk with God because we often walk into places which do not profit us. But if God takes the lead we will profit from every step. Walking with God requires submission. Our walk with God also requires trust. Walking with God appears to imply co-equality but this is not necessarily the case. A lot of this walk with require us to follow him in humility and reverence. God can become a friend to us but he is also a master and a father. "A son honoureth his father, and a servant his master: if then I be a father, where is mine honor? and if I be a master, where is my fear? [Mal 1:6]"

God has walked through all the paths within creation and He knows all of the names of the streets He has paved. So we must walk with God in humility and trust. We must follow God and then God will follow us. This is a secret which was communicated to the disciples in the gospel of John. "Then Peter, turning about, seeth the disciple whom Jesus loved following [Jn 21:20]." If we learn to follow the principles of Christ then the spirit of Christ will learn to follow us. Walking with God requires obedience. When we are disobedient we feel guilty and believe that God no longer wants to walk with us. This is what happened with Adam and Eve after they disobeyed God. After doing so they "hid themselves from the presence of the LORD God amongst the trees of the garden [Gen 3:8]." But God is faithful and merciful. Rebellion will result in God leaving us and walking with another. But when we choose to repent and confess our sins, God is faithful to cleanse the dirty footsteps we have trodden upon the floor, and he is more than able to set us in a clean place before his sight. Enoch could walk with God for so long because he was obedient. It is our obedience therefore which will enable us to walk with God continuously. Enoch had a great faith in the LORD and this faith was expressed with his continual obedience.

Walking requires steps to be taken. Each step is important for God. It is the steps which define the path we walk in: and we will find that God is just as interested in the steps that we take than he is in the overall journey. This is because the journey is composed by a combination of steps. These steps are steps of either obedience or disobedience. The small steps are just as important to God as the large lunges and marathons. We must therefore be obedient in the small day to day decisions than we are with the even bigger ones. If we cannot obey God in smaller commandments such as keeping our environment tidy or working hard when we are at work how will we be able to obey God for the more challenging commandments in life, such as forgiving those who hurt us and praying for those who despitefully use us and despise us?

There are a number of things we must obey in order to walk before God. We will discuss these over the course of this text.

Interested in The Nature of God

The best of marriages are built upon the foundation of friendship rather than carnality. Some couples rush into marriage because of sexual attraction. But these marriages rarely last for too long because there is no foundation of commonality between the two. It is not good to generalise. Some of these relationships do last. But when the common attraction begins to simmer it becomes clear between the two parties involved that there was less in common than was first thought.

This is in contrast to marriages built upon friendship. Sexual attraction is temporary whereas friendship can be eternal. Sexual pleasure only lasts for a moment of time or two but the pleasures received from a good friendship transcends the sphere of carnality and time. By extension: marriages to God which are motivated by carnal desires and material gain do not last too long. But if we want to walk with God because we desire his friendship and his counsel then we will find our walk with God to be successful and long lasting.

We walk with other people when we are interested in discovering more about their nature. If two people do not share any common goals then they will rarely decide to walk with one another. But if two individuals are interested in knowing one another in a more intimate way then they will become motivated to spend more time with one another. We will only want to walk with God when we decide to devote our lives to knowing Him. A woman who is only interested in what her husband provides for her will only want to spend time with him when he is giving her something in return. But a woman who is interested in knowing her husband intimately, placing his friendship far above all of the material blessings and sexual pleasures he provides for her, will desire to spend all of her time with him. God has called us to be the intimate woman. The bride of Christ who is loyal and faithful during all circumstances. The woman who has a sincere desire to know him and to hear his voice at all times. Jesus says that these are they who thirst and hunger for righteousness. They are not content with feeling the presence of God sometimes but they want to be surrounded by Him at all times. They do not want to walk with him once a week but they are devoted to walking with him at all times.

Enoch learnt a tremendous amount about God whilst he walked with him for 300 years. The more time we spend with somebody the more we will learn about their nature. This is why having a daily devotion time is crucial. We spend devotion time with God by setting apart some time during the day to pray, worship, read his word and meditate. Enoch would have had a good devotion life. He may not have had a bible but he must have spent a considerable amount of time communicating to God.

Enoch was not satisfied with spending a few hours here and there seeking God. He loved the presence of God so much that he decided to devote his whole life and being to God. This is what it means to walk with God. This is what it means to be holy. It means to travel with God wherever you go.

Devotion time is a good way to begin our relationship with God. But the only concern with setting a daily devotion time is that it may become ritualistic and we may only focus on God during these set periods of time; only to then forget about God for the remainder of the day. Enoch was not content with just sitting with God for a couple of hours each day but Enoch wanted to walk with God every hour of the day. If Enoch only spent a few hours of the day walking with God then there would have been only so much that he could have learnt each day. But if he spent all of his day walking with God he would have learnt much more and become even more intimate with him. Enoch was clearly very hungry to know more about God. Enoch therefore devoted his whole day focusing upon God. He was addicted to speaking to God about anything and everything.

The knowledge of God is progressive and there is more to learn about him each day. This is why Moses, even at the age of over 80, was pleading with the LORD to see more of his glory [Exo 33:18]. Moses had seen many things which God had done. Moses spoke to God "face to face, as a man speaketh unto his friend [Exo 33:11]" and yet he was still desperate to know more and more about God. "And Moses said unto the LORD . . . Now therefore, I pray thee, if I have found grace in thy sight, shew me now thy way, that I may know thee, that I may find grace in thy sight [Exo 33:12-13]." Moses had seen God in the burning bush, he had witnessed his spectacular and fiery descent from heaven upon mount Sinai, he had regularly spoken to him in the midst of the cloud in the Tabernacle, and yet he sincerely yearned to discover more and more about the Ancient of Days.

We can never know too much about God. After all this is the God who has overseen the steps of all civilisations. He is the God who created all of the constellations and calls them by their names. He is the God who knows things high up, as high as the highest heaven and his wisdom is deeper than the deepest pit of hell. He is unsearchable and His knowledge and understanding cannot be limited by any man. He knows the end before the beginning. There is nothing too difficult for Him to achieve. He is One God and He is perfectly unique.

Is this not a Being whom any wise and inquisitive person yearns to discover more deeply?

We should always be motivated therefore to discover more about his many truths. Jesus said blessed are they who hunger and thirst after righteousness for they shall be filled. God will also fill us up with his knowledge if we hunger after his presence and continue to read his Word. But first we must be like the Apostle Paul and confess that we hardly know anything at all, even if he has already shown us many remarkable things in the past.

"Brethren, I count not myself to have apprehended: but this one thing I do, forgetting those things which are behind, and reaching forth unto those things which are before, I press toward the mark for the prize of the high calling of God in Christ Jesus. [Phi 3:13-14]"

This is why Jesus says that the kingdom of God is like children. When we walk in humility and concede that there is still so much more to learn about God than we already know, then we will always be able and open to absorb much more which He has in store for us to receive. But if we proudly attest that we have already attained all knowledge and human virtue then we will not feel motivated in the slightest to seek him any more.

Enoch

Friendship With God Vs The World

The name Enoch has a few meanings: it means "dedicated," "initiated" and "disciplined." Now there are two Enoch's which are spoken of in the book of Genesis – two Enoch's which lived remarkably stark and different lives. The first Enoch which is mentioned is Enoch the son of Cain [Gen 4:17]; but the second Enoch, son of Jared, which we hear of later, is far more significant for our studies at this time.

According to common folklore, the first Enoch, son of Cain, is attributed as being one of the first founders of occult magic. During these very same days "the sons of God saw the daughters of men, [Gen 6:2]" and had worryingly descended unto the Earth during this time. And according to the book of Enoch [the later one who walked appropriately with God], it were these very same fallen angels who taught them how to construct weapons of warfare; make-up, the cutting of roots and witchcraft; astrology and enchantments – and so on and so forth [Eno 8]. Enoch, son of Cain, was said to be very learned in the discipline of these forbidden sciences – and freemasons and John Dee, who was said to rediscover the Enochian language [which is the language of the fallen angels] lay testament to this historical belief. Enoch means "dedicated," or "initiated" – and this Enoch was no doubt dedicated and whole-heartedly disciplined towards his secret profession. But let us not waste time discussing the life of the profane – and let us delve deeper into the beloved Enoch of God, he who was rewarded for his diligent and disciplined relationship with the Lord. For whilst Enoch, the son of Jared was "initiated" into the discourse of sacrilegious and forbidden knowledge – we have another Enoch who was initiated into the many holy secrets contained within the third heavens.

In the book of Jasher we are informed of how "Enoch was wrapped up in the instruction of the Lord, in knowledge and in understanding; [and that he] wisely retired from the sons of men and secreted himself from them for many days [Jasher 3:2]." We may first comment upon the fact that there were no bibles during Enoch's day, no written Law and no heavenly priests or pastors – and Enoch lived a few hundred years before the wicked times of the great deluge. All of his understanding, knowledge, and wisdom was passed onto him personally from the Lord himself – and his intimacy with God is just a testament of how "dedicated," and "disciplined" he was to seek for nothing but his mysterious voice . . . Enoch was in many ways, besides Moses, a true predecessor of Jesus; in that he symbolised the perfect individual who is so desperately eager to consistently seek that face of the most High God.

In order to seek the face of God he necessarily departed from the world and "wisely retired from the sons of men." This is because the sons of men were far too busy preoccupied with the world: far too busy concerned about their wives and children; far too busy concerned about their finances and businesses; yea, all of the sons of men were far too busy concerned about this new technological advancement or this new worldly creation or song. "A little leaven leaventh the whole lump [Gal 5:9]," so the more time he would have spent entertaining the worldly customs of his friends, the less time he would have correspondingly spent pursuing the spiritual things which belong to Christ.

"Love not the world, neither the things that are in the world. If any man love the world, the love of the Father is not in him. For all that is in the world, the lust of the flesh, and the lust of the eyes, and the pride of life, is not of the Father, but is of the world. And the whole world passeth away, and the lust thereof: be he that doeth the will of God abideth for ever [1 Jn 2:15-17]."

The more time spent in the world, the less time one can spend with a jealous God who admittedly exclaims he is at enmity with the world. Enoch, who was the first anointed after Adam, did not need to join a large congregation or church to heed the WORD of God. He was not taught and 'initiated' into these divine discourses by a preacher, pastor or even a book – but such was his insatiable desire, daily, that the Lord eventually impressed his sacred presence into his life.

"the anointing which ye have received of him abideth in you, and ye need not that any man teach you: but as the same anointing teacheth you all things, and is truth, and is no lie, and even as it hath taught you, ye shall abide in him [1 Jn 2:27]."

Now, "Enoch wisely retired from the sons of men." He did not need any intermediary, besides the holy spirit himself, to know "the deep things of God [1 Cor 2:10]." His heart was set on pleasing God. He was hungry to please God so he spent alot of time with Him alone. He did not wait upon anybody to compel him or command him to follow God but he purposed in his heart to make intimacy with God as his one main priority in life.

When Jesus Christ needed God he did not call on his disciples to follow him; but he went out into the mountains or the wilderness to pray and worship by himself. And even when he required their assistance in the garden of Gethasamene – for such was his grief and tribulation during this brief period of time – did not all of his closest friends abandon him and fall asleep during duty? Enoch could have been led astray by following anybody else in his pursuit to walk with God – so once he had made the bold decision to discover as much of the Lord as was permitted for to him to do – he boldly abandoned all of the worldly concerns which could have distracted him, and he diligently sought to maximise the opportunity of hearing his voice.

"He that loveth father or mother more than me is not worthy of me [Matt 10:37];" he that loves girlfriend or wife or even children more than God, is not a worthy subject for the Lord. The heart cannot be divided when you serve the most High. If it is divided you will be like Adam and disobey the LORD when it comes to very significant decisions which also affect others. Enoch retired from all men and did not have the competing whispers of wife, children or friends to deny the attention he devoted to the Lord of Spirits.

"he that is married careth for the things that are of the world, how he may please his wife [1 Cor 7:33]."

Enoch understood that the pleasure, beauty, joy and peace which he shared with the Alpha and Omega could not be compared to the joy he could otherwise share with his closest companions here on the earth. Enoch understood that everything in this world is like a temporary illusion – the lust of the eyes, the flesh and the pride of life were all destined to pass away – but "whosoever does the will of God [1 Jn 2:15] [that is to glorify him in holiness]" would "receive manifold more in this present time, and in the world to come life everlasting [Lk 18:30]."

Enoch was not a friend of the world but was a friend of God alone. The same can be said for Jesus. Enoch was translated and taken into heaven; and so can the same be said for Jesus. Enoch knew who Jesus was, as the anointed holy one who is surrounded by the cheribum, and Jesus took Enoch up into heaven to foreshadow the destiny of his end-time Saints:

"For the Lord himself shall descend from heaven with a shout, with the voice of the archangel and with the trump of God: and the dead in Christ shall rise first; Then we which are alive and remain shall be caught up together with them in the clouds, to meet the Lord in the air: and so shall we ever be with the Lord [1 Thess 4:16-17]."

Now we must ask ourselves a number of pertinent questions, questions which shall not doubt trouble the heart, but questions which shall certainly enable us to know whether we are in Christianity for the right reasons or not. Many of us have good jobs, a loving wife, family and friends – a comfortable home and status in this world – I am sure all of these gifts provide us with a decent level of satisfaction. But is this the life the Lord wishes us to ultimately fulfil; or do you not think that our jealous Lord, who calls Himself our husband, requires us to spend most of our energy and focus upon his work alone? The saint must be willing to dispose of everything if he is to eventually walk the narrow path of redemption. The LORD does not change, and neither does His WORD, so because the world has changed need not mean that the LORD requires us to abandon worldly pursuits in order for us to follow Him to New Jerusalem. Elijah was another prophet who had abandoned all of the world for the lonely pursuit of the LORD. When he met Elisha to anoint him as his successor this is what occurred:

"So he departed thence, and found Elisha the son of Shaphat, who was ploughing with twelve yoke of oxen before him . . . and he left the oxen and ran after Elijah and said, let me kiss my father and my mother, and then I will follow thee [1 Kings 19:19-20]."

If Elisha, the wealthy merchant and herdsman of Israel can immediately abandon all to follow the spirit of Elijah, how much more should we abandon all to follow the walk of Jesus Christ? When we read through the gospels there were many individuals who abandoned their worldly lives to walk alongside Jesus. "The people sought him, and came unto him, and stayed him, that he should not depart from them [Lk 4:42]." The same can be said for the twelve disciples and the same can be said for Levi [who later became Matthew]. But all of these people witnessed first-hand the glory of the God incarnate; and the same can be said for Elisha who had heard of the many miracles of Elijah.

We as carnal human beings often wish to follow something we can interact with with our own hands and eyes . . . we also often love the very things which are discerned in the physical realm. But when Jesus was walking upon the earth he gave many of his disciples the opportunity to love him and wisely follow his steps to inherit his many blessings. But what about we who have not seen Jesus Christ? Enoch had not seen Jesus Christ during the beginning of his path – and he certainly did not follow any other prophet to begin his relationship with Christ – so why must we be allured and persuaded by the evidence of physical things? We must remember to walk "by faith and not by sight [2 Cor 5:7]" and we must also remember the words of Jesus who after his resurrection acclaimed to "Thomas, because thou hast seen me, thou hast believed: blessed are they that have not seen, and yet have believed [Jn 20:29]."

Not only do we believe in the ascension of Jesus Christ, but we also believe – just like Enoch – that there is no better life than walking hand in hand with the most High God. We must also believe some of the more serious and testing words, such as the need to love Jesus above all of the world, and also the announcement that "it is easier for a camel to go through an eye of a needle, than for a rich man to enter into the kingdom of God [Matt 19:24]." These words were spoken to the rich young ruler who had carefully followed and adhered to the law of Moses. But when Jesus told him to sell all he had and to give his money to the poor we are told of how "he went away sorrowful for he had great possessions [Matt 19:22]." God will test us all to see whether we can abandon any earthly idol to follow him and help his angels alongside the harvest of the earth. This is the only way for us to prove whether or not our love for Him is genuine. The LORD may not necessarily desire you to abandon all for his cause at this very moment of time; but we must be fellowshipping with Him daily to gain both the confidence and experience of his incomparable love and peace. We must love his WORD, that is Jesus Christ, more than anything else in this world – and we must hunger and thirst for his presence on a daily basis. Only then shall we be emboldened to depart from the shadows of this world, and only then shall we, like Enoch, "wisely depart from the sons of men" to one day be translated into heaven just like Jesus Christ. As was mentioned before, Enoch knew of Jesus Christ, and let me leave you with one of his vivid encounters he shared of Him in a book which was said to be written by him:

1. And it came to pass after this that my spirit was translated And it ascended into the heavens: And I saw the holy sons of God. They were stepping on flames of fire: Their garments were white [and their raiment], And their faces shone like snow.

2. And I saw two streams of fire, And the light of that fire shone like hyacinth, And I fell on my face before the Lord of Spirits.

3. And the angel Michael [one of the archangels] seized me by my right hand, And lifted me up and led me forth into all the secrets, And he showed me all the secrets of righteousness.

4. And he showed me all the secrets of the ends of the heaven, And all the chambers of all the stars, and all the luminaries, Whence they proceed before the face of the holy ones.

5. And he translated my spirit into the heaven of heavens, And I saw there as it were a structure built of crystals, And between those crystals tongues of living fire.

6. And my spirit saw the girdle which girt that house of fire, And on its four sides were streams full of living fire, And they girt that house.

7. And round about were Seraphin, Cherubin, and Ophannin: And these are they who sleep not And guard the throne of His glory.

8. And I saw angels who could not be counted, A thousand thousands, and ten thousand times ten thousand, Encircling that house, And Michael, and Raphael, and Gabriel, and Phanuel, And the holy angels who are above the heavens, Go in and out of that house.

9. And they came forth from that house, And Michael and Gabriel, Raphael and Phanuel, And many holy angels without number.

10. And with them the Head of Days, His head white and pure as wool, And His raiment indescribable.

11. And I fell on my face, And my whole body became relaxed, And my spirit was transfigured;
    And I cried with a loud voice, ...with the spirit of power, And blessed and glorified and extolled.

12. And these blessings which went forth out of my mouth were well pleasing before that Head of Days.

13. And that Head of Days came with Michael and Gabriel, Raphael and Phanuel, thousands and ten thousands of angels without number.
    [Lost passage wherein the Son of Man was described as accompanying the Head of Days, and Enoch asked one of the angels as in 46:3. concerning the Son of Man as to who he was.]

14. And he (i.e. the angle) came to me and greeted me with His voice, and said unto me:
    'This is the Son of Man who is born unto righteousness, And righteousness abides over him, And the righteousness of the Head of Days forsakes him not.'

15. And he said unto me: 'He proclaims unto thee peace in the name of the world to come; For from hence has proceeded peace since the creation of the world, And so shall it be unto thee for ever and for ever and ever.

16. And all shall walk in his ways since righteousness never forsaketh him: With him will be their dwelling-places, and with him their heritage, And they shall not be separated from him for ever and ever and ever.

17. And so there shall be length of days with that Son of Man, And the righteous shall have peace and an upright way In the name of the Lord of Spirits for ever and ever.'

Enoch Chapter 71

These are the types of visions and encounters we shall receive when we forsake the glory of this perishing earth. This is the type of prestige and honour that we shall receive, "for ever and ever and ever" if we shall walk the narrow path of Jesus Christ. This is the type of love and acknowledgement from the Highest Himself we will gain when we come to put the Alpha and Omega above any of the base idols found on this earth. All praise and Honour belongs to the Mystery, the LORD God of Hosts for ever and ever. Amen.

Two Types of Knowledge

God is calling every saint into deeper intimacy. This was the intention of God from the beginning and it remains so today. We become intimate with God by spending personal time with him in the secret place. Not only be studying his word but also by communing with him in prayer, meditation and worship. We become intimate with him by subduing our flesh and letting his Spirit work through us. We become intimate with him by clinging unto our faith in the Lord Jesus Christ and by continually confessing his name. We basically become more intimate with him when we obey all of his commandments and love him with all of our heart, soul, might and mind.

God is calling us to have an experiential knowledge of Him. It will not suffice for us to have an intellectual knowledge of him alone. Having an intellectual knowledge of God is not bad in itself but God is calling us to have a more experiential knowledge of him too. This is because the experiential knowledge of God is better than the intellectual.

Consider the following. If I was boy who had been raised in a foster home then I might have known about my real dad despite never meeting him. Maybe my foster parents had told me many stories about him and perhaps I had read about his life in some diary entries. These second hand accounts helped me to gain an insight into his character and the personal events of his life. However, I would not have really known who my dad was until I meet him personally and discovered his character for myself.

The same applies to God who is my Father in Heaven. There are many people who have heard about God. They understand that he is omnipotent, omnipresent and omnibenevolent. But have they experienced all of these characteristics for themselves? It is one thing to hear about God from another person but it is entirely different thing to hear about and experience God for yourself. It is one thing to see God sanctify and work himself through another person but it is another thing altogether to see God sanctify and work himself through you.

Moses The Man of God

The difference between those who know God intellectually and those who know God experientially is exemplified to us in the life of Moses and the children of Israel.

"He made known his ways unto Moses, his acts unto the children of Israel [Psa 103:7]."

God taught Moses his ways because the prophet had a solid and unquestionable relationship with Him.

"And the LORD spake unto Moses face to face, as a man speaks to his friend [Exo 33:11]."

Moses had set up the tabernacle after the children of Israel had fashioned for themselves a golden calf. God descended upon the tabernacle and waited at the door. Everybody in the congregation knew that it was Him because He descended upon the tabernacle in a cloudy pillar. But they only waited at the door and were not able to enter into the holy place of the Tabernacle where He dwelt. God only spoke to Moses whilst the remainder of the people witnessed the sign.

"And all the people saw the cloudy pillar stand at the tabernacle door: and all the people rose up and worshipped, every man in his tent door [Exo 33:10]."

Whilst the congregation stood at the door of their tents on the outskirts of God's presence, Moses stood at the door of the Tabernacle in the immediate presence of the LORD.

In the book of Numbers the author reiterates God's familiarity with the prophet Moses. Miriam and Aaron were unhappy about Moses's marriage to an Ethiopian woman so they gossiped behind his back and sought to discredit his ministry. God had heard their complaints and he came down in a pillar of cloud to voice his own take on the issue. The

LORD defended his servant Moses and He revealed His sore displeasure about the accusations which were made by Aaron and Miriam.

"And he said, Hear now my words: If there be a prophet among you, I the Lord will make myself known unto him in a vision, and will speak unto him in a dream. My servant Moses is not so, who is faithful in all mine house. With him will I speak mouth to mouth, even apparently, and not in dark speeches; and the similitude of the Lord shall he behold: wherefore then were ye not afraid to speak against my servant Moses?" [Num 12:6-8]

When God rebuked Miriam and Aaron he told them that Moses was his faithful friend. Although Miriam and Aaron were both prophets who had received great authority amongst the congregation they had not yet attained to the same level of intimacy which their younger brother Moses had come to share with the LORD.

This encounter teaches us three important lessons.

(1) We should never be quick to speak badly about somebody for a decision they have made when we do not and cannot know the precise nature of the relationship they share with God. God may have allowed Moses to take this woman to be his wife – the scripture does not clarify exactly, but we do not have any evidence to suggest that God opposed the union. This is why it was foolish for Miriam and Aaron to oppose Moses's decision. It is easy to judge others when we think they have made a mistake but that is not our responsibility but the responsibility of Christ, especially when they have not overtly sinned. If we are to judge or rebuke somebody in the body of Christ we can only do so from a place of love and edification. We should not accuse them and speak badly of them behind their back, but we must approach them and speak to them individually to address any sincere concern which we may share about their spiritual development. We should never accuse somebody in a position of leadership, when in doing so it only helps to boost our ego. We should never rebuke a God ordained leader because we feel insecure about our own position which God has given us. We

should never be quick to judge somebody when we cannot quite discern the motives of their heart. It is difficult but we must do our best to remember that the Lord does not see as a man sees: that whilst a man looks at the outward appearance, the Lord looks at the heart [1 Sam 16:7].

(2) The second lesson we can learn from this episode teaches us about different levels of intimacy different people share with God. There is no limit to how close we can become with God and everybody has a different level of intimacy with the LORD. This means that some people are closer to God than others. God can use us to be his prophet or to hold any other office in the ministry but this does not necessarily mean we are intimate with God. Aaron and Miriam had a relationship with God but it was not as intimate as the relationship the LORD shared with his servant Moses. With Aaron and Miriam He spoke to them in dreams and appeared to them in visions but with Moses He spoke to him face to face. When we are closer to God he will speak to us in simple terms and less frequently in dark speeches and parables. If God did this with Moses then he can certainly do this with us. It is God's desire to have more friends upon the earth as he had with Moses. It should be the desire of every saint to speak and hear from the LORD as a man does from his friend.

We should not be quick to dishonour somebody who has a closer relationship with God than us. Some may feel inspired to do so in order to exalt themselves. If there is somebody who you know who shares a close relationship with God and they are struggling with some type of sin it is wise to pray for them and to intercede on their behalf. Rebuke not an elder [1 Tim 5:1]. It is also wise to submit yourself under their mentorship so that you might learn how to develop your relationship with the Father too. But never gossip and accuse them because the LORD will not leave you altogether unpunished.

(3) The third lesson is to do with the retribution of the LORD. When we have a close relationship with God He will fight all of our battles even if we do not see who it is who is attacking

us and discrediting our work. The LORD will bless those who bless you and he will curse those who curse you [Gen 12:3]. This is the inheritance of the servants of the LORD. When Miriam and Aaron were murmuring against their brother, Moses did not even initially know but the LORD did. God brought their accusations to light and punished Miriam by striking her with leprosy in the sight of all the congregation. There is nothing which is hidden which shall not be revealed. God will not only reveal those who are plotting against you or speaking badly of you but he will also punish them too. Look at what happened to David's wife Michal. She spoke badly against the man of God because he was dancing in the sight of the LORD. She envied him and despised him in her heart because she knew God had given him great favour as a result of their close relationship. Not only was she rebuked by the king but God also struck her with a barren womb as a consequence of her accusations. When we have an increasingly intimate relationship with God he will also strike all of our opponents with a curse: they will be barren and will never be able to bear good fruit.

Moses Sought Intimacy

There are different levels of intimacy we can share with God. There is a difference between witnessing God's works and being a witness of the work God does inside of you. You can witness what God does in the external world, what he does through other people and what he does in the natural world, but this is tremendously different to being a witness of the miraculous work which God can do on the inside of you. Moses was a witness of the external and internal works which God performed during his era whereas many of the children of Israel only witnessed what God did in the open, in the natural world.

Moses became intimate with God because he was committed to knowing more about God. When you are committed to a cause you will exhibit consistency and you will spend most of your time pursuing that one particular goal. Moses was naturally an inquisitive man. But Moses focused and channelled his inquisitive nature towards the pursuit of God. There are a number of men in this world who are also very inquisitive. They love knowledge and wisdom too. But not all of them are inquisitive about God. Moses was successful in his pursuit of knowing God because he devoted his entire life to seeking the face of God. His eye was single and he devoted his whole life to deepening his depth of intimacy with the living God.

It is one thing to be inquisitive about the riches of God's knowledge but it is another thing to sacrifice everything to focus upon claiming it for yourself. Knowing God requires sacrifice. We must be willing to forget and forsake anything and everything which prevents us from becoming more intimate with God. This is what can be understood as the law of specialisation. If we want to specialise in anything we must focus on that one particular study and neglect the study of anything else which is not conducive to our overall aim. This is what professional academics do. They initially have a broad knowledge of a number of disciplines which come under a particular study. A humanities teacher may have a good understanding of religion, history and geography. But an excellent academic will narrow his focus to only one discipline and even within this discipline he will only focus on one particular subject. He will therefore come to neglect the other broad studies and now specialise in one particular discipline. So a humanities academic may one day choose to specialise in Religious studies and even within this discipline he may choose to specialise within Old Testament poetry. This will produce a greater degree of understanding in his chosen field.

This is how Moses was with God. He had a good upbringing and had studied many of the traditions of the Egyptians within the royal palace.

"And Moses was learned in all the wisdom of the Egyptians, and was mighty in words and in deeds [Acts 7:22]."

But when he reached the age of 80 and God appeared to him in the burning bush Moses now made the decision to specialise in one thing: his spiritual ascent towards God. Moses's priority was not to lead the people of God to the Promised Land, although God had called him for this specific purpose. Moses's priority in life was to know God.

Whatever we decide to prioritise in this life is what we will come to excel in the most. Moses excelled in the pursuit of God because he made it his *only* priority. This does not mean Moses did not have other responsibilities. He certainly did because he was a father as well as a husband and a mighty judge and leader. But all of these titles and roles did not prevent him from pursuing his number One responsibility and desire; seeking and knowing God.

We have other responsibilities in life too. We may have secular jobs, God may have given us a responsibility for a ministry and we may have work to do in our families. However, our number One concern in this life must be seeking the face of Jesus Christ and knowing Him experientially. Our number One concern in this life must be seeking God in his Word and obeying him during every moment in this life.

The Burning Bush

An inquisitive individual will always learn something new. God is always looking to reward inquisitive people: those who continually question the nature of his being and seek to discover hidden knowledge and wisdom found within him.

"God looked down from heaven upon the children of men, to see if there were any that did understand, that did seek God [Psa 53:2]."

God is assuredly a rewarder of those who diligently seek Him and he has promised us that we will seek Him and find Him when we seek for Him with our whole heart [Jer 29:13]. He will never turn away the person who seeks him with the whole heart. God values an inquisitive person just as much as a teacher who values a student who always completes their homework and arrives to lessons on time. An inquisitive person will neglect all of the affairs of the world to focus on God and to receive answers in his word.

Moses was a very inquisitive person.

"And when he was full forty years old, it came into his heart to visit his brethren the children of Israel [Acts 7:23]."

Moses went to visit his brethren for a number of reasons but one of the main reasons was because he was inquisitive. He wanted to inspect their wellbeing.

Moses also showed his inquisitive nature when he saw the burning bush. Moses could have been fearful, he could have ran from the sight of the strange sign but when he saw the sight of the burning bush he was intrigued by it and decided to investigate it.

"And Moses said, I will now turn aside, and see this great sight, why the bush is not burnt [Exo 3:3]."

God was pleased by Moses's inquisitive approach. In fact, the scripture lets us know that God only decided to speak to Moses *after* he walked towards it and sought to investigate it.

"And when the LORD saw that he turned aside to see, God called unto him out of the midst of the bush, and said, Moses, Moses. And he said, Here am I [Exo 3:4]."

When we are inquisitive towards the LORD and continue to approach him in the secret place, then God will speak to us just as he did to Moses. Moses did not need to investigate the sight. He could have fled the scene and reported the sign to Jethro and his household. But Moses approached the sight because he knew God must have had a part to play in it, He was very hungry to discover more about his grace and he latched onto the opportunity which had finally been provided for him. This was a life-changing experience which he knew would have changed his life. He took it and despite his fears he drew closer to the burning bush which symbolised the purifying nature of God.

He was inquisitive, yes by nature, but by this time Moses had now learnt to cultivate and focus all of his attention towards the pursuit of knowing God. When he approached the burning bush God spoke to him and called him by his name. This reveals how God knew him already and wanted to initiate a personal relationship with him. God is also a burning bush which cannot be consumed. He desires for us to approach him inquisitively and he will reward us when we do so. He will call us by our names and initiate a personal relationship with us when we seek him.

We should never be afraid to seek the LORD. The author of the epistle to the Hebrews exhorts us to come boldly, not fearfully, before his throne of grace that we might obtain mercy and find grace to help us in the time of our need [Heb 4:16]. He is always available to us no matter where we are or no matter what time we may desire his assistance. This is why it is wise to "Seek ye the LORD while he may be found, call ye upon him while he is near [Isa 55:6]." We may wish to ask when is the LORD near and when can he be found. The answer is NOW. In this transitory stage which we call life, before we die, and our spirit returns unto the Father.

The episode of the burning bush was likely the first time Moses had spoken to God face to face despite hearing of Him a number of times through oral tradition. He had heard about his patriarchs Abraham, Isaac and Jacob and maybe he had studied about the nature of the Almighty God before. But this was likely the first time he had heard the voice of God.

Logos and Rhema

"As he drew near to behold it, the voice of the Lord came unto him [Acts 7:31]."

There is a big difference between hearing the voice of the Lord and hearing the word of God. We can hear the word of God when it is spoken on the pulpit or when we read it from our bibles. But when we hear the voice of God we hear the tone, sound and volume of the living God speaking directly to us. This too is possible in our relationship with God.

The difference between the two is distinguished by the two Greek words which are designated for the English word 'word.' In English there is only one word for 'word.' But in Greek there are two: Logos and Rhema. Logos refers to the written word of God, the oracles of the holy prophets and Apostles which are recorded for our own comfort in ink and on paper through the inspiration of the Holy Spirit. Rhema refers to the instances when God speaks to us personally, when we hear his voice. An example of this would be when the angel of the LORD appeared to Gideon. Gideon was told by the angel that the children of Israel would be freed from the captivity of the Midianites but when Gideon first heard this he was full of unbelief. Gideon replied to the angel "where be all his miracles which our fathers told us of, saying, did not the LORD bring us up from Egypt? [Jud 6:13]" The oral history which Gideon heard from his father was the logos but the word he was now hearing from the angel was the rhema.

Moses too received the Logos of God. But when he turned aside to see the sight of the burning bush he heard the rhema of God. This reveals that we hear the voice of God when we spend more time seeking him in the secret place. Both Moses and Gideon heard the rhema when they were alone in the secret place.

God can speak to us in a number of ways but no way can be as efficient and meaningful than hearing his voice personally. Paul in his epistle to the Romans declared that faith comes by hearing and hearing the word of God [Rom 10:9]. The word which Paul uses for 'word' in this instance is rhema. Faith comes from hearing the living word of God and not necessarily the logos of God. Many muslims are well versed with the scriptures, so are many Jews, as the case example of the Apostle Paul before his conversion serves to show us. However, they still lack faith in the promises made by God. They still lack faith in the man who was sent into the world to redeem mankind from their sin. This is because their hearts have not been cut and convicted by the Sword of the Spirit. The Sword of the Spirit is the word of God. This was wielded by Peter on the day of Pentecost. He was full of the Ghost and preached the word of God as the Spirit led him. He did not try to convince them through the bible (although there is a time and place for this too). But he simply preached whatsoever the Holy Ghost gave him utterance to speak. And here was the result:

"Now when they heard *this*, they were pricked in their heart, and said unto Peter and to the rest of the apostles, Men *and* brethren, what shall we do?" [Acts 2:37]

The NIV states that "they were cut to the heart." When God speaks to us through his rhema word then he speaks to our hearts rather than our minds.

It is the living word which is activated by the Spirit of God which gives man faith and not the dead letter. The living word of God is the Rhema. "For the letter killeth, but the spirit giveth life [2 Cor 3:6]."

He can speak to us through dreams, with an audible voice, through prophets and seers, through his word the holy bible, through his Son in heaven, through nature and little children, through the circumstances we face in life, through other members in the body of Christ, through visions and images we receive in deep prayer, he speaks to us in so many different ways. No man can say God does not speak to us. But we must show ourselves determined and consistent to receive his counsel daily, especially if we desire to hear his voice audibly.

It took Moses a very long time for him to achieve this. But his testimony is here to encourage us into the reality that we too can receive this great gift which is birthed from a place of deep intimacy. The rhema of the LORD does not always need to be heard in a loud audible voice. Sometimes you can hear it in a small still voice as it was in the case of Elijah.

For instance, although I have heard the LORD speak very clearly to me in two occasions upon waking up out of my sleep, most of the time when I hear the rhema of the LORD he will almost whisper a word or two into my spirit. I have heard words such as 'diligent,' 'process' and 'commended' and these words have served to inspire me to research and conduct a bible study on these topics. Now I believe they came from the LORD because the Holy Ghost dwells on the inside of me and it is written that the Spirit of the LORD bears witness with our own spirits that we are the children of the Living God. If we believe we are the children of God then we must also be confident that God speaks to us daily. In my experience of seeking the LORD I have found this to be the case. God speaks something new each day, even if it may be only one word; he is always wanting to teach us something new every day. The best way that I discern that the word is coming from the LORD is when I receive the word on more than two occasions. If I keep hearing the specific word or sentence and it compels me to study the word in relation to the bible so that I might become edified and increase in the stature of Christ then I am certain that the word is from the holy Ghost and not from some unclean spirit. For example there was one day when I heard the word 'commended' more than at least five times during the day. This lead me to a bible study about commendation and I was lead to 2 Corinthians 10 where the Apostle Paul says "For not he that commendeth himself is approved, but whom the Lord commendeth. [2 Cor 10:18]" God was teaching me a lesson during this time and he was encouraging me with his own commendation for my ministry.

Rhema is useful in our lives because it gives us specific and clear instructions to follow in any given circumstance. Rhema is also important because it is a personal word for us during a given day. It therefore enables us to know the times and seasons we are going through in a particular stage of our life. For example if I hear the Lord tell me "excellence" then I will discern that God is calling me to prepare for a life of excellence in every aspect of my life.

Not all the words which God gives us are easily discerned. Some are more elusive and will take more time for us to understand. But if we seek the understanding with great hunger then we will surely discover the meaning.

The logos is important too because it gives us the principles and commandments we must follow to obey God. It is the collection of heavenly wisdom which sages, prophets, priests and Apostles have received from the one true God through their respective walks with the LORD. But the Logos can occasionally lack specific and personal commandments which we need during specific times. If I had to choose between two jobs then the bible may lack the answer. But if I received a prophetic word from the LORD he would be able to guide me. Or if there were two women whom I wanted to marry and both of them were godly individuals in accordance to the prescriptions outlined in the bible how could I make my choice unless it be from the rhema word of the Lord? Rhema gives us answers and personal solutions to some specific concerns which are not clearly outlined in the scriptures or which we may lack present knowledge of. For example, when the Apostle Paul was given a thorn in his flesh and buffeted by the messenger of Satan he was perplexed and could not find any answer. He sought the Lord thrice to receive an explanation and the Lord gave it to him with rhema.

"And he said unto me, my grace is sufficient for thee: for my strength is made perfect in weakness [2 Cor 12:9]."

Rhema also provides us with specific instructions which help to improve the effectiveness and efficiency of our ministry. In the book of Acts God told Philip to "Arise, and go toward the south unto the way that goeth down from Jerusalem unto Gaza, which is desert [Acts 8:26]." God told Philip to do this because he wanted him to preach the gospel to an Ethiopian Eunuch who would later become converted and baptised. Ethiopia as a result of Phillip being able to hear God's voice later become the first country in the world whose Monarch would openly endorse Christianity.

But God will only speak to us if we are prepared to listen to him, even if at first his commandments seem pretty strange. Although God told the disciples to go throughout the whole world to proclaim the gospel there was a time when the Holy Ghost forbade Paul from going to Asia to preach the gospel [Acts 16:6]. This may have seemed strange at first but the LORD only spoke to Paul because he knew he was going to listen. God speaks to all people about judgment and the need for repentance, even if he foresees that they will not change, but he only does this because this is a fair position to take and because he genuinely wants all people to be saved. But God will only speak clear and progressive, daily messages to those whom he knows will listen to Him. For what would be the point of continuing to speak to somebody if He knew we would never listen? If God wanted you to fast for 21 days and he knew you would continually reject his request, do you think he would continue to speak to you? God could foresee that Abraham would sacrifice his son Isaac so he spoke to him and commanded him to do so. God stopped speaking to Saul when he anticipated that the King had made the choice to continue living in rebellion [1 Sam 28:6]. But God began speaking to David when he discerned that this was a man after His own heart, a man who would delight to do His will [Acts 13:22].

When God can see that we will obey whatever he asks us to do then he will speak to us more often and clearly. This is why God spoke to Philip. Philip obeyed immediately and ventured out into the desert despite the harsh conditions he was destined to encounter. After the Eunuch was baptised by Philip, the evangelist was teleported by the Spirit of God away from the region. This shows us that the rhema will always provide us with a greater efficiency to continue carrying out the work of God [Acts 8:26-40].

Everybody has the ability to prophesy and hear from God.

"For ye may all prophesy one by one, that all may learn, and all may be comforted." [1 Cor 14:31]

But the person who occupies the office of a prophet is particularly more sensitive to the voice of God.

Rhema is the reason why prophets are so sought after. Rhema is also the reason why Paul advised the Corinthian church to covet the gift of prophesy above all other gifts. A prophet is particularly sensitive and better positioned to receive the rhema from God. Most of the logos in the bible is the rhema which was received by a prophet of God at a historical period of time. So when we read Isaiah 53 for example this is the logos of God. But when Isaiah heard it from God and scribed it down, it was rhema for him. A prophet has the ability to hear directly from the Spirit of God. This is a gift every sincere Christian must crave in order to become more effective in combating the kingdom of darkness. When we hear from God more clearly we will also be more edifying towards the saints in the body of Christ. "He that prophesieth edifieth the church [1 Cor 14:4]."

How do we grow in rhema?

- Study the word of the Lord regularly. "Study to shew thyself approved unto God, a workman that needeth not to be ashamed, rightly dividing the word of truth." [2 Tim 2:15] When God speaks most of the time he will confirm what is already in the bible. If you do not know the word, then it will become more difficult to discern whether and when God is speaking to you or not.
- Wait upon God in meditation. "Rest in the LORD, and wait patiently for him: fret not thyself because of him who prospereth in his way, because of the man who bringeth wicked devices to pass." [Psa 37:7] It is easier for you to discern the voice of God over your flesh or over the whispers of the spiritual adversaries when your mind is focused upon God's word.
- Remain attentive to what God is saying during prayer. It is always useful to wait upon God in silence after you have spent some time in prayer and worship. What can you see? What words can be heard in your inner man. The voice of God often sounds like your own voice.
- Covet earnestly the gift of prophecy. Receive it through faith. Become more familiar with prophetic people or plant yourself in a prophetic church.

Dependence

One of the most important keys we must possess to maintain a healthy relationship with God is dependence. This is when we depend upon God for everything that we do. For what we say, what we do, where we go, who we marry, who we choose to befriend, where we decide to live, where we believe God is calling us to work, the list really is endless for those who have learnt to completely yield themselves in complete dependence to God's will.

Jesus Christ teaches us of our need to remain completely reliant upon God. Jesus Christ was evidently dependent upon God during the entire span of his life. Jesus Christ was dependent upon God for everything. We know that this was true because he said he never sought his own personal will but the will of the Father [Jn 5:30]. If we seek our own will for our lives without seeking the will of the Father then we are clearly not dependent upon God. But if we say to God not mine own will, but let your will be done in my life Father, then we are exhibiting the marks of complete dependence.

Jesus Christ always exhibited perfect dependence upon God. "My meat is to do the will of him that sent me, and to finish his work [Jn 4:34]." Jesus Christ always sought the will of the Father, even when he was facing harsh persecution. There were times when he suffered greatly for complying with the will of God for his life but he never once complained or threatened to rebel. When he was praying in the garden of Gethsemane, shortly before his betrayal, he cried out to his disciples that his soul was exceedingly sorrowful, even unto the point of death. Jesus did not want to endure such a terrible death. He did not want to leave his disciples at such an early stage of his life. He did not want to be delivered into the hands of sinners who he knew would mistreat him unfairly. But he still cried out sincerely to God in prayer,

"O my Father, if it be possible, let this cup pass from me: nevertheless not as I will, but as thou wilt [Matt 26:39]."

Jesus had the opportunity to escape when the chief Priests and Pharisees arrested him. His disciple Peter was determined for his master to escape. He did not want his beloved to die so he struck one of the officers on the ear with his sword.

Jesus was not best pleased with his disciple.

"Thinkest thou that I cannot now pray to my Father, and he shall presently give me more than twelve legions of angels? [Matt 26:53]."

Jesus was making it clear to his disciples that he could have evaded the hands of his enemies if he had so desired. He had the authority and the power to call down multitudes of angels. But Jesus chose not to do so because this was not the will of the Father. Jesus depended entirely upon what God wanted for his life and so he waited patiently for the Father to move on his behalf.

"When he was reviled, reviled not again; when he suffered, he threatened not; but committed himself to him that judgeth righteously." [1 Pet 2:23]

To depend upon God means to commit your whole life to Him as a living sacrifice. Those who depend upon God offer up there body as a living sacrifice unto Him, living a holy life which is acceptable unto God. They are not conformed to this world but they are transformed into the image of Christ by renewing their minds with his word regularly. They trust in God and in all of his promises. They understand that there is a very great reward for their dependence upon Him.

Jesus Christ was dependent upon God because he completely trusted in Him. Jesus understood that God is the only Person who is good [Mk 10:18]. And because he believed this he also understood that everything God would will would also be good too. God is love. Therefore everything which God decides to do in our lives stems from a place of love. God is our Father and he knows what is best for us even if we must endure suffering along the way.

"Now no chastening [suffering] for the present seemeth to be joyous, but grievous: nevertheless afterward it yieldeth the peaceable fruit of righteousness unto them which are exercised thereby [Heb 12:11]."

Jesus Christ was dependent upon God because he knew that He is all-powerful, all-wise and all-knowing. He understood that if he was to rely upon himself he would not have been able to succeed in anything at all. But because he relied upon the source of all success, the source of all power and authority, he was only destined to excel upon the earth before dying and later ascending into heaven.

When we look at all the success stories in the Bible—the figures like Abraham, Job, David, Daniel, Paul and Peter—we see one common thread running through all of their lives; they relied upon the LORD for the success they walked in. God is a God of success and excellence, He is a God of might and of miracles, and once you walk with Him daily it becomes impossible for you to not excel in life. This is why Jesus said "the Son can do nothing of himself, but what he seeth the Father do: for what things soever he doeth, these also doeth the Son likewise. [Jn 5:19]" Everything which Jesus accomplished was motivated and influenced by the Father. He sought to emulate the Father and exhibit his nature in everything that he did. This could only take place if he learnt, which judging by his results he did, to depend upon having an intimate relationship with God.

"It is the spirit that quickeneth, the flesh profiteth nothing: the words that I speak unto you, they are Spirit, and they are life [Jn 6:63]."

When we rely upon our own strength, intellect and wisdom we will not be very successful in the work of God, no matter how talented or hard-working we may be. "Except the LORD build the house, they labour in vain that build it: except the LORD keep the city, the watchman waketh but in vain [Psa 127:1]." We won't make many genuine converts. And we will not be able to obey God and live in sincerity of love by our own strength. We cannot love or forgive our enemies without the help of God. We cannot raise the dead or heal the sick unless we depend upon Him. This is because "the flesh profits nothing [Jn 6:63]." This is because without God we are merely dust. Remember Adam was made out of the dust of the earth but it was not until God breathed his Spirit into the lifeless body that he then became a living soul. We too are lifeless unless we receive the Spirit of God. We cannot do anything substantive or enduring unless we rely upon God's Spirit in the process. When we rely upon the Spirit of God we will not only overcome all obstacles but we will also achieve the impossible. We will live a supernatural life just like Jesus did.

This is nothing new. The flesh has always been weak. The flesh has always been at enmity to the law of God. It has always been resistant to the will of God. And we understand that a man cannot do any righteous work unless it is God who is working through him to execute His own righteousness through him [Phi 2:13]. Only God is good. So if Jesus is good then this is because God is inside of him. Only God has life and if Jesus has life inside of him it is because God has given him this life. "For as the Father hath life in himself; so hath he given to the Son to have life in himself [Jn 5:26]." God has all power and Jesus has this power because he has received it from the Father. "And Jesus came and spake unto them, saying, All power is given unto me in heaven and in earth [Matt 28:18]."

If we are not good then this is because God is absent from us. If we do not abide in God then it is impossible for us to be righteous. This why we must depend upon God in all things. We must depend upon God because he is the only wise, loving and powerful Being. Anybody who is deficient from God is deficient from his attributes. But when God works inside of us, through us, and upon us, then we receive the divine attributes of His Almighty Being. We will be wise; we will be loving; we will be powerful and we will be so only by virtue of God's Spirit which works within us. This is the notion of grace. We cannot strive independently [that is to say without the assistance of God] with our own flesh in order to become righteous, wise or full of love. But through the grace of God, which we receive by faith in the gospel, we can receive his divine nature and walk like Jesus. Jesus Christ depended upon God because he understood how the LORD was the source of all his good works. Jesus Christ knew this and testified of this fact a number of times:

"The words I speak unto you I speak not of myself but the Father who dwelleth inside of me he doeth the works [Jn 14:10]."

Jesus depended upon God for everything he did. Even the words which he spoke were spoken by God whom dwelt on the inside of him.

God was the Spirit and Jesus Christ was the son, the flesh and body which the Father had fashioned so that he might dwell upon the earth and communicate to his people. Jesus never spoke a word of his own accord. He never wasted any words which his Father did not motivate him to speak. He did not use any idol words. Just like Samuel he did not let any of his words fall to the ground [1 Sam 3:19].

Jesus did not do any work which his Father did not inspire or command him to do. Jesus was very careful to do only those things which his Father had permitted him to do. Jesus completely submitted to and depended upon God.

To depend upon somebody means to lean and rest upon the assistance of another. If I say I depend upon you then I am basically saying two things. (1) That I trust you and (2) that I need you to assist me in anything that I wish to do. Therefore, Jesus Christ trusted in God so deeply to such an extent that he was willing to depend upon Him for everything he achieved. He never once sought to achieve anything by his own wiles: but he relied upon God for all. This is what it means to be completely yield to God. This is what it really means to say and walk in the realisation that "I and my Father are one [Jn 10:30]." It is therefore our dependence upon God which enables us to express the fullness of God's majesty upon the earth.

Dependence results in unity. God said that Adam would leave his father and mother and cleave to his wife [Gen 2:24]. He said Adam would stop leaning upon his parents and become one with his Wife as he cleaved [and depended] upon Eve. Jesus Christ calls us to do the same thing with him. He wants us to take his yoke and become married to him. To marry means to join together; to combine harmoniously. Unless we do so with Christ we cannot find any success in this spiritual life. Without him we cannot do anything meaningful for God at all [Jn 15:4]. Just as the branch depends upon the vine so that it might bear fruit; no more can we bear any spiritual resemblance to God unless we abide and depend upon Christ. This dependence requires continual faith in the Lord Jesus. This means that we literally believe Jesus is indeed at the right hand of the Father and that he has the ability to come into contact with us whenever we seek him. We cannot depend upon something we do not believe in. But if we believe him to be who he says he is then it would be wise for us to depend upon him in all things: seeing that he is love and that he has our very best interest in his heart.

In every word, action and motive that Jesus Christ had, he relied upon the Father. Jesus would often say he could do nothing of himself, and he would frequently emphasise that in everything that he did do, he had to rely upon his Father.

"Then answered Jesus and said unto them, Verily, verily, I say unto you, The Son can do nothing of himself, but what he seeth the Father do: for what things soever he doeth, these also doeth the Son likewise." [Jn 5:19]

Jesus's judgment and morality was based upon God's judgment and morality, and not his own.

"I can of mine own self do nothing: as I hear, I judge: and my judgment is just; because I seek not mine own will, but the will of the Father which hath sent me." [Jn 5:30]

"My doctrine is not mine, but his that sent me." [Jn 7:16]

"For I have not spoken of myself; but the Father which sent me, he gave me a commandment, what I should say, and what I should speak." [Jn 12:49]

A young child is completely dependent upon their parents. Everything which pertains to their nourishment and sustenance is provided for them by their parents. They cannot do anything of themselves. This is how Jesus was with God. Jesus said we must become like little children to enter into heaven [Matt 18:3]. A large part of this refers to our need to remain dependent upon God. If we do not learn to depend upon God then how can we be called his children? If we do not learn to depend upon God then we will not receive the inheritance he has preserved for us but we will be seen as illegitimate heirs like Ishmael.

We must learn to depend upon Jesus. We can do this by remaining obedient to him and by following his commandments from a place of rest. We need to also be sensitive to the direction of his Holy Spirit. If we do not depend upon Jesus then we will not have a fruitful life. Jesus goes into great detail to emphasise this in in the gospel of John when he says:

"Abide in me, and I in you. As the branch cannot bear fruit of itself, except it abide in the vine; no more can ye, except ye abide in me. I am the vine, ye are the branches: He that abideth in me, and I in him, the same bringeth forth much fruit: for without me ye can do nothing [Jn 15:4-5]."

Jesus makes it clear that we can do nothing unless we first learn to depend upon him. This does not mean we can do nothing at all but it means that we can do nothing to please God unless we learn to do it by abiding in Christ.

We abide in Christ by depending upon the Spirit of God. When Jesus Christ said "I and my Father are one [Jn 10:30]" what he really meant is that I am One with the Spirit of God. The Spirit of God is the life and animation of God. The life and Spirit that is in God was made manifest in the flesh of Jesus Christ and God has promised us the very same gift by our faith in his crucifixion and resurrection. "For as the Father hath life in himself; so hath he given to the Son to have life in himself [Jn 5:26]." God has given us this life too "and this life is in his Son [1 Jn 5:11]." We received this life—which is the Spirit of God— when we believed in the Lord Jesus Christ. "He that hath the Son hath life; and he that hath not the Son of God hath not life [1 Jn 5:12]." If we remain in the faith then we will remain obedient. And if we remain obedient then we will remain dependent on him through his holy Spirit. This is because God has given his holy Spirit to those who obey him [Acts 5:32].

When we have faith in Jesus we will have an unction from the Holy Ghost. But God is calling us to depend upon the Holy Ghost in everything that we do. What we speak, how we walk, how we behave around other people — God wants us to rely upon his Holy Spirit for everything that we do in the remainder of our lives. The Spirit of God is like a still small voice which is always motivated by love. God is love so anytime we do not act from a place of love we are sure to know that God is not involved.

Although we are sealed with the Holy Ghost we can still decide to act in such a way that grieves Him. This is when we do not yield to His influence and inspiration and choose to act in a carnal way which is contrary to his perfect will. Jesus Christ always yielded to the Spirit of God. This is how it was possible for him to never sin. There were times when his flesh was weak but he always chose to yield in submission under the hand of God. This means that the option is open for us to do likewise.

When we learn to yield to the Spirit—during every moment of the day—then we will show how it is possible to completely depend upon God. This should be our aim everyday. The main reason why we do not equal the works of Christ is because we often fail to depend upon God for everything. Sometimes we do not depend upon God because we feel that our gifts and talents will suffice. There is only so much our gifting can do. But when we rely upon the Spirit of God we will always have so much more success. Bezaleel the son of Uri was a gifted and talented artisan. But he could not build the tabernacle until God filled him with the spirit of wisdom, understanding and knowledge in all manner of workmanship [Exo 31:3]. Saul was a man who was intelligent, hard-working and diligent. He was a naturally gifted man. But when Samuel anointed him and the Spirit of the LORD came upon him he was "turned into another man [1 Sam 10:6]." Jesus Christ was another talented man who grew in stature and in wisdom from a very young age. But Jesus did not begin to manifest his many signs, wonders and healings until he was baptised in the river Jordan and the Holy Ghost descended and abode upon him from heaven. From that time forward Jesus Christ depended upon the Holy Ghost *entirely* and he was led by God in everything that he did.

In the book of Acts Jesus told the disciples to wait in an upper room in Jerusalem until they were endued with the Holy Ghost from on high. Jesus told the disciples they would receive power after the Holy Ghost came upon them and they would then become witnesses for him both in Jerusalem, and in all of Judea and Samaria even unto the uttermost parts of the earth [Acts 1:8]. Despite being used by the Lord prior to his ascension for a number of signs and wonders, even casting out demons and healing diseases, Jesus did not send the disciples out to witness about his resurrection until they received the Holy Ghost. This showed that they could only work for him effectively after they had learnt to depend upon the presence and power of God.

When we depend upon God we will always ask him for the best line of action to take. This is something which David knew of well. David was a man who typically made inquiries to God before he made big decisions [1 Chron 14:8-17]. He did this because he had learnt to trust and depend upon God's judgement. Jesus Christ also made a number of inquiries before making a big decision. This was most notable when he decided to pray all night before choosing his 12 disciples [Lk 6:12-16]. Jesus did not choose them but God chose them for His own purposes. We must also learn to make inquiries from the LORD before making any significant decision. We may not always get answers straightaway but if we persist in patience, even as Jesus Christ did by praying for an entire night, then God will certainly give us the answer we require.

When we depend upon God we will also be comfortable with sharing our concerns with Him. We will confess our sins to Him more often and we will regularly request to receive move grace to strengthen us in time of need. It is important for us to cast our care upon Him because He cares for us [1 Pet 5:7]. All of us have concerns which we want to cast away. Sometimes we may be quicker to cast them upon another person before we first resort to casting them upon God. If we depend upon God first and foremost then we will always receive better assistance. It is better to cast our cares upon God because it is better to depend upon God than any other being. This is because God can alleviate, eradicate and uplift us from any problem far better than anybody else could. Dependence upon God will therefore always yield better results than depending upon self or other people who are by nature limited.

"Not by power, nor by might, but by my Spirit says the Lord [Zec 4:6]."

Fruit of Dependence

Dependence is the opposite of independence. When we are independent we will use our own strength, might, intelligence and whatsoever skill we may have been endowed with upon birth in order to excel. But when we are dependent upon something or somebody we will realise that we cannot excel by our own gifts and talent alone; but that we must depend upon the helping hand of another to make us victorious. When we are independent we are like an unmarried woman. But a dependent person is like a married woman who relies upon her husband. An independent, unmarried woman cannot produce children by herself; but a married and dependent woman has the potential to produce legitimate children. When Moses received the covenant laws from God he was told that a husband must provide his wife with raiment, food and a home [Exo 21:10]. This means the wife depended upon her husband for her basic needs. When she became married to her husband she began a covenant with him. She became one with him. She was no longer one with herself but she now became one with another. Does not the same apply to us when we depend upon Jesus? We will no longer be self-sufficient but we will become dependent upon him who gives us all holiness and power.

God made humans to depend upon one another. Families are built and sustained by dependency. When God created Eve it was said that a man should leave his father and his mother to cleave unto his wife: that they would become one flesh [Gen 2:24]. Any man when he was younger would have depended upon his parents. For all children depend upon their parents. But God was letting future generations know that a man could not always remain dependent upon his parents. When they were old enough to marry they would leave the dependence of their parents and now cleave to their wife. They would therefore transfer their dependence upon their wife. The wife would depend on the husband and the husband would depend upon the wife. They would no longer be twain but one flesh.

This means Jesus Christ depends upon us. Not only do we depend upon the Lord Jesus but Jesus also depends upon us. But the way a husband depends upon his wife is different to the way a wife depends upon her husband. Eve depended upon Adam for direction, mobility, leadership and sustenance. Whereas Adam depended upon Eve for help in his work, companionship and for child-bearing. The same applies for our dependency upon Christ and his dependency upon us. For he is the husband and we are his wife. Jesus depends upon us to help him establish his kingdom upon the earth. When Adam came upon the earth God gave him a job to do in tending the garden of Eden. Eve was created in order to help him. When Jesus Christ came upon the earth he was given a job to do by establishing the kingdom of God upon the earth. God has created the bride of Christ in order to help him [Jesus] accomplish this.

"For we are his workmanship, created in Christ Jesus unto good works, which God hath before ordained that we should walk in them [Eph 2:10]."

When we are dependent upon our own strength we make ourselves independent from the help of God's hands. Everybody is dependent on something or someone. Some are dependent upon their jobs, others are dependent upon wealth while some others are dependent upon their mothers and other family members and friends. Everybody has something and someone who they tend to depend upon.

Dependence in God will result in independence from the world. "Where the spirit of the Lord is there is liberty [2 Cor 3:17]." God sent Jesus Christ into the world so that we could learn to depend upon God alone. In our dependence upon Christ we receive genuine independence. This is an independence from other people and selfish habits which do not necessarily profit us. "If the son therefore shall make you free, ye shall be free indeed [Jn 8:36]." "If ye continue in my word, then are ye my disciples indeed; and ye shall know the truth, and the truth shall make you free [Jn 8:31-32]."

Jesus Christ gives us independence from the dependence of pernicious habits and persons which serve to undermine our standing with God. I used to be dependent upon drugs. I used to be dependent upon fornication and pornography. I used to be dependent upon the opinions of my fellows. I depended upon a number of worldly means to acquire peace, happiness and stability. None of these means provided me with the peace, joy and stability I so desired. Any semblance of pleasure which I derived from them were only temporary at best. But Jesus Christ set me free from my dependence upon them. And now I am dependent upon him. It is my dependence upon Christ which gives me true independence from those things which harmed my soul.

The issue of idolatry is closely tied to dependency. God said we cannot serve mammon and God. In other words we cannot depend upon God and depend upon money: we either learn to depend on one or the other. This is why Jesus said it would be difficult for us to enter into the kingdom of God if we trusted in riches. Jesus is teaching us to depend on him and him alone; and only be doing so will we be able to endure in the faith.

Adam and Eve depended upon one another. Adam depended upon Eve for children and for service and Eve depended upon Adam for direction and leadership. When two people depend upon each other they become one. When we depend upon Jesus we become one. And when we are one in Jesus we are one in God. "He that is joined unto the Lord is one spirit [1 Cor 6:17]." We are one with Jesus Christ by virtue of the Holy Spirit which rests within us. God wants us to become entirely dependent upon the Holy Spirit in everything that we achieve. When we are dependent upon the Holy Spirit we are consequently dependent upon God.

We are either working by our own spirit or by the Spirit of the LORD. God is calling us to submit to his Spirit so that he can work through us to execute his plans upon the earth. "Thy will be done on earth as it is in heaven." In the book of Ephesians Paul says the wife must submit to the husband [Eph 5:22]. The bride of Jesus Christ must subsequently submit to her husband. To submit means to yield to a superior force or to the authority or will of another person. When we submit to God we are depending upon him. Our submission to him will result in God's Holy Spirit working through our tabernacles. If God works through us we will be much more successful than we could ever be by our own means. A wife can achieve much more when she is working in partnership with her husband. There is only so much she can achieve by herself. She can produce children when she is one with her husband but when she is alone she cannot achieve much.

In the beginning "God blessed them, and God said unto them, be fruitful and multiply [Gen 1:28]." He told "them." He did not tell Adam alone. He did not speak to Eve alone. But "God said unto them." The wife cannot produce children alone and neither can we be fruitful alone. It is clear that she needs her husband to produce fruit and so must we. We must be one with Jesus Christ to remain fruitful. But this requires utter dependency and submission upon God. We submit to God when we obey him. "And why call ye me, Lord, Lord, and do not the things which I say? [Lk 6:46]" We submit to God when we continue to sincerely say "not my will Lord, but let your will be done Lord."

We have to depend upon God for salvation too. We are not saved by the works of the law, by our own righteousness or by our own good works but we are saved by our dependence on the blood of Jesus Christ and the regeneration of the holy Ghost.

The scriptures reveal the necessity of this dependence in a number of symbols. We are likened to children, brides and sheep in a number of places in the gospels. All of these beings are dependent upon a higher authority. A child is dependent upon their parent; a wife upon her husband; and a sheep upon their shepherd. We are God's children, God's wife and God's sheep - we must therefore depend upon him at all times.

When we depend upon Jesus we will be found one in God. This means that dependence will transform our identity. Everything which Jesus owns will also be given to us. Jesus Christ is called the word of God. He is also called the son of God. When we are one in Jesus Christ we will also be called the word of God. We too will be called the sons of God. Dependence upon God brings great gain. It will require sacrifice: for if we suffer with Christ we will also reign with him [2 Tim 2:12]. But when we depend upon Jesus we will freely receive everything which he currently owns. This is all things. For Jesus has all dominion upon earth and the heavens. "He that overcometh shall inherit all things; and I will be his God, and he shall by my son [Rev 21:7]."

Jesus Christ is God in the flesh. If we are in Jesus Christ then we are also God in the flesh. This is because the same Spirit which is inside of Jesus is also the same Spirit which is inside of us today. The same Spirit which hovered upon the waters in the opening passages of Genesis is the same Spirit which we have freely received by grace. And the same power which framed the worlds and fashioned the heavens of old is the same Power which resides within us today. The same Spirit which rose Jesus Christ from the dead is the same Spirit we have received today by faith.

Jesus Christ said we are gods [Jn 10:34]. This is true. We are the images of the invisible God. We are his tabernacle and his temple. We are the body of the Almighty God. Man cannot see God unless they see us. Without us they will not know or see God. God made man in his image and in his own likeness. But then came sin through Adam. Jesus Christ came to restore everything man had lost and to bring him back into the likeness of the Father. Man is the conduit of God. He is the physical vessel which houses the Spiritual fullness of God. For there are some vessels of righteousness and other vessels of unrighteousness. Notwithstanding you are all gods.

God told Moses "I AM." He reaffirmed to Moses, just in case the prophet did not know, that he was the source of all being and consciousness. Jesus Christ said "before Abraham was, I am [Jn 8:58]." This was the Father speaking in the Son. The same "I AM" which was in Jesus Christ is the same "I AM" which is inside of you. This is God's being, God's nature, God's Spirit. If Jesus said "I am the way, the truth and the life," so can you. Not because you are any better than Jesus, or not because you have worked to be like Jesus, but solely because you have received the fullness of Jesus through faith. The Jesus that is inside of you will always testify of Jesus and not of self. This is because the Jesus that is inside of you is the Holy Spirit. "But when the Comforter is come, whom I will send unto you from the Father, even the Spirit of truth, which proceedeth from the Father, he shall testify of me [Jn 15:26]."

One of the first things Jesus does in our lives is transform our identity. We no longer identify with self but we now identify with the nature and being of God. The old man was crucified on the cross with Jesus Christ and the life we now live is identified with the nature of the resurrected Christ. God literally moves into our lives and parks his presence into our bodies. This is what baptism communicates. We are dead to self and alive to God through our dependence upon Christ. We now become the wisdom, the righteousness, the holiness of God. Our old identity is buried under the ground and the resurrected Jesus Christ is alive in us to work through us. This new man that lives inside of us is Jesus Christ. God does not change himself when he abides in us but he is the same yesterday, today and tomorrow. This means we receive his immutable nature when we are born again. Although we may be beset by many external changes and oppositions which we will invariably face, we still fundamentally remain the same inside. This is what it means to say that we have received the seal of the Holy Ghost. Jesus Christ said when we listen to his word and do it then he will liken us to a wise man who dug deep and built his foundation upon a rock. The house is immovable even when floods, winds, earthquakes and other temporary cataclysms threaten to engulf it. "Heaven and earth shall pass away but my word will endure [Matt 24:35]." Our personality will one day die but the personality of God which is inside of us will remain forever. When we identify this with this personality and become rooted in its Spirit then we will remain in glory forever, even as Jesus Christ remains glorified forever.

"And, Thou, Lord, in the beginning hast laid the foundation of the earth; and the heavens are the works of thine hands: They shall perish; but thou remainest; and they all shall wax old as doth a garment; and as a vesture shalt thou fold them up, and they shall be changed: but thou art the same, and thy years shall not fail [Heb 1:10-11]."

"The man who is wholly sanctified is so drawn towards the Eternal, that no transitory thing may move him, no corporeal thing affect him, no earthly thing attract him. This was the meaning of St Paul when he said, *I live; yet not I; Christ liveth in me.* Now the question arises what is sanctification, since it has so lofty a rank. Thou shouldest know that real sanctification consists in this that the spirit remain as immovable and unaffected by all impact of love or hate, joy or sorrow, honour or shame,

as a huge mountain is unstirred by a gentle breeze. This immovable sanctification causes man to attain the nearest likeness to God that he is capable of. God's very essence consists of His immovable sanctity; thence springs His glory and unity and impassibility. If a man is to become as like God as a creature may, that must be by sanctification."
[Meister Eckhart, Sanctification]

Humility

A quality deeply related to dependence is humility. We are humble when we realise that we are nothing without God. We are humble when we recognise that we could do no good thing unless it is God working through us to do good. And we remain humble when we continuously return to God in prayer to help us offset the pressures of life which beset us daily. Without God we could do no good thing. But only humility can help us to appreciate this fact.

The opposite of humility is pride. Prideful behaviour deludes man into believing that he needs no help from God. The prideful man relies upon his own strength, his own beauty, his own wisdom and wealth.

"Lo, this is the man that made not God his strength; but trusted in the abundance of his riches, and strengthened himself in his wickedness [Psa 52:7]."

He is certain that his own gifts and blessings are sufficient for him to excel in life. He does not need a saviour. He does not even think about salvation. "Salvation from what?" he will sneer in pride. His pride has corrupted his wisdom. His pride has blinded his vision so that he can no longer see. In his pride he was welcomed humanism and atheism. He once used to believe in God but his pride has corrupted and twisted his intuition. In their profession of wisdom, they became fools. It was pride which was the seed and the fruit thereof was folly.

Pride makes us ignorant and foolish. Humility has the opposite effect: it fills us up with wisdom and understanding. This is because humility will draw us into the presence of God who freely provides us with every spiritual blessing in heavenly places. Whereas pride draws us away from God, closer to the devil who is the author of all confusion and lies. God will always resist us when we are too proud no matter how knowledgeable we may be.

When we have a humble heart we will depend upon God in all things. We will quickly understand that we need God in all things to excel. It is pride which compels man to make every significant decision without the green light from God. Maybe man believes he can make a better decision than God. Or maybe man believes he can rely solely upon his own strength or will-power to succeed in life. Or maybe man believes God does not even care. Either way this is not the wisest option to take. God knows what is best for us and what is adverse for us in life. He sees the end from the beginning and does not want any of us to face unnecessary shortcomings in life. This is why it is wise to consult God before every decision. We can do this through prayer and patience as we await an answer.

But this requires humility on our part. If we are prideful we will believe our decisions will always be the best. We will likely neglect good advice from friends and family and we will rely upon our own intelligence and experiences to circumnavigate our lives. Prideful people will shun good advice and inexorably reject criticism. But when we are humble we do otherwise. We recognise that our own intelligence and experiences in life are limited. We recognise that there is only so much we know and there is only so much that we can experience in this short life-time. It is therefore wise to gain counsel from other people who are better equipped to provide a solution to a problem you face. But only a humble person will realise and concede this. This is why humble people turn to God during adversity. They understand that it is only God who can bring man out of a miry clay. They also appreciate how it is only God who can empower any meaningful and durable success. "For is God that worketh in you both to will and do of his good pleasure. [Phi 2:13]" "Except the LORD build the house, they labour in vain that build it: except the LORD keep the city, the watchman waketh but in vain [Psa 127:1]."

When we do receive advise, correction or counsel from somebody we must always ensure that it lines up with the word of God. If it does, then it certainly comes from God.

"I the LORD speak righteousness, I declare things that are right [Isa 45:19]."

But if it does not then you do not need to follow it. Not all advice comes from God and not all counsel is for your edification or good. Some advice is sent by the devil and it is given to you in order to divert you from God's plans for your life.

A good example of this would be the case of Rehoboam who became the King of Israel after his father Solomon had died. When he replaced Solomon on the throne he faced a lot of opposition from the Northern tribes who had explained to the king that the taxation rates which were legislated by his father were too excessive and unfair. Rehoboam told the people to return in three days so that he could seek counsel and decide upon the next course of action.

The first step was wise. We should never feel rushed into making an important decision. We must first seek advice and always pray to God before deciding what to do next.

Rehoboam sought counsel from two types of people: his younger and more familiar friends, and his elder counsellors who had been with his father Solomon during his prosperous reign. Rehoboam went to the elders first and they gave him reasonable advice. "And they spake unto him, saying, If thou be kind to this people, and please them, and speak good words to them, they will be thy servants for ever [2 Chron 10:7]." Rehoboam rejected the counsel of the elders and consulted his friends instead: those who had grown up with him from youth.

"And the young men that were brought up with him spake unto him, saying, Thus shalt thou answer the people that spake unto thee, saying, Thy father made our yoke heavy, but make thou it somewhat lighter for us; thus shalt thou say unto them, My little finger shall be thicker than my father's loins. For whereas my father put a heavy yoke upon you, I will put more to your yoke: my father chastised you with whips, but I will chastise you with scorpions." [2 Chron 10:10-11]

The advice Rehoboam received from his friends was clearly unreasonable. Nevertheless, he chose to follow it and refused to listen to the obvious despair of the people. The consequence of this decision was dramatic and swift. The children of Israel rebelled and seceded from Rehoboam. They became a sovereign state and set up Jeroboam to reign in his stead. As a result, Rehoboam was now the king of only 2 tribes, Judah and Benjamin, and the other tribes of Israel remained "in rebellion against the house of David to this day [2 Chron 10:19]."

It is humble when we ask for counsel from somebody. But we may not like the advice we receive even if it is the best line of action to take. It therefore requires even more humility for us to follow good advice even when we do not necessarily want to follow it. If we ask for advice then reject it because the advice does not necessarily agree with our initial standpoint then this is prideful. Being humble requires us to embrace counsel and decisions which we do not necessarily agree with at first. We may not see the benefit of following somebody else's counsel at first but it takes humility to trust their experience and wisdom, in light of ours, before we act upon it and later see the value of the advice they gave us. Humility is about lowering yourself. Saying to yourself "I do not always know what is best." Humility involves admitting that you need help from another being to excel.

Jesus Christ was a humble man. Jesus Christ did not understand why he had to endure so much agony in the garden of Gethsamene. He complained to his disciples and told them how his soul was sore vexed and exceedingly sorrowful. He did not want to follow through with what he foresaw in the Spirit. He knew the extent to which he had to suffer and he wanted God to ease the pain. But Jesus said to the Father "let your will be done and not mine." Jesus remained humble even when he did not understand, even when he did not want to follow it, and he submitted himself under the counsel of God. "He humbled Himself and became obedient to the point of death, even the death of the cross [Phi 2:8]."

Humility is a requirement for obedience. We cannot be obedient unless we are first humble. Jesus understood that God knew best and that He alone was the source of all goodness and good counsel. Jesus was therefore always obedient to the word of God. Satan tempted him many times and sought to undermine his obedience but Jesus remained humble. "Not as I will, but as you will [Matt 26:39]." These are the words of a man who abides in humility. He knows that what God wills will always be perfect in comparison to what he wills.

When we disobey God we are basically telling him that our line of action is better than what he has already commanded us to do. Eve ate from the tree of knowledge because it looked good to the eyes, looked good for food and because it was desirable to make her wise. But when she disobeyed she reaped the fruit of her disobedience, which was death. Solomon is another example. He was greatly disadvantaged in later life because of disobedience. God had warned the children of Israel not to multiply wives unto themselves. But Solomon loved many strange women. Solomon knew the importance of remaining humble. He spoke of its importance a number of times in his Proverbs. But Solomon disobeyed nevertheless. Maybe he did not see any problem or foresee any danger in multiplying wives for himself. But God understood why. Because they eventually led his heart astray from God and he began serving false idols. Solomon must have grown proud because of his success in early life. It is so easy for us to become proud when things are going well for us. When this happens it inevitably results in disobedience. This is what happened in the life of King Uzziah who had a very successful beginning to his reign over Judah. "But when he was strong, his heart was lifted up to his destruction: for he transgressed against the LORD his God, and went into the temple of the LORD to burn incense upon the altar of incense [2 Chron 16:16]."

God forbids certain actions because he knows what is best for us and he understands why certain decisions will result in adversity and in some instances irreversible damage. This is why he commands us to abstain from certain actions and decisions. When we reject the commandments of God we therefore show Him that we believe we know better. This is not humble but prideful. A man who is disobedient is therefore a prideful man. But a man who is always obedient is always able to remain humble.

Humility is the realisation that you cannot make good decisions by yourself. Humility is the understanding that you need good counsel and assistance before you excel in any area of your life. Humility is the appreciation that there always remains somebody who is higher and better than you. Humble people read a lot of books and listen to a lot of counsel. They are quick to hear and slow to speak.

Moses was a man who was very humble. He was described as the meekest man on the earth during his ministry. Moses was meek because he was aware that God was the source of all of his might. He had spent a lot of time with God and was a recipient of much of his grace. Moses understood that everything which he owned was freely given to him by God. When Moses heard the angel of the Lord in the flaming bush this was because of the grace of God. When God used Moses to split the Red Sea this again was because of God's grace. And when Moses face shone like the sun it was not because he was glorious by his own strength or virtue but because he had spent plenty of time with God on the holy mount. Everything Moses achieved was because of the grace of God. Moses acknowledged this and continued to walk in the awareness of this fact. This is why he was meek, this is why he was humble: because he knew that it was God who was working through him to give him the spirit of excellence in every area of life. A humble person is therefore somebody who is forever aware of God's grace in his life. He never thinks that he has accomplished or achieved something by his own ability or strength but in everything he remains thankful to God who he knows has empowered him to become victorious.

Pride Is A Deterrence

A prideful spirit will deter unbelievers and believers from approaching you. A prideful person will often think that he is better than other people. This is not a positive character trait to have: and it does not make you relatable or approachable to others who will certainly be able to discern this trait upon you. Anybody can discern whether somebody is prideful or meek. We can discern it in the way that they conduct themselves and a prideful person will likely have a haughty facial expression. According to Solomon one of the things which God despises is a proud look [Pro 6:17]. God is not the only person who despises a proud look but so do we!

Most of the people in the world do not have the Spirit of God abiding upon them, but this does not necessarily mean that they cannot recognise the basic attributes of our character. In the book of Genesis we are told that Potiphar knew that God was with Joseph [Gen 39:3]. We hear of a similar story with Abimelech and Abraham [Gen 21:22]. This shows us that even unbelievers can recognise when God is with us or not. Similarly, they can also discern whether we are prideful or not. If we are prideful then the chances are that they will not seek to approach us much. Rather than attracting them to the gospel we will actually be putting them off. This is because there is something about pride which makes somebody very unapproachable. But being meek has the opposite effect: not only will God be comfortable around you but other people will also want to learn from you too.

Jesus was very meek. This made him very approachable to the thousands of people who decided to follow him at the various stages of his successful ministry. Jesus, to the disbelief of the scribes and Pharisees, typically ate with sinners and publicans [Lk 5:30]. They would often invite him into their homes to learn about his principles and to spend time eating with him. In one memorable encounter, the Lord was invited by a Pharisee called Simon into his home for a meal. Whilst they were eating a woman who was a sinner entered into the home unexpectedly. "When she knew that Jesus sat at meat in the Pharisees' house, she brought an alabaster box of ointment [Lk 7:37]." The woman was so overwhelmed to meet the gracious Messiah that she began to weep and wash his feet with her tears. She proceeded to kiss his feet and then she anointed them with the oil.

The Pharisee who invited the Lord was understandably shocked and confused. "He spake within himself, saying, this man, if he were a prophet would have known who and what manner of woman this is that toucheth him: for she is a sinner [Lk 7:39]." The truth is that the Lord knew exactly who she was. But there was something about his aura - something so gentle and humble - which made him so much more approachable than other people. He came to call the sinners to repentance and he treated all people equally. This made him so approachable to all types of people. If he was proud like the Pharisee he would have said something along the lines of "do not touch me because you are an unclean sinner." But because he was humble and lowly he was willing to embrace all manner of people.

This is what Jesus said to all those who considered following him: "Come unto me, all ye that labour and are heavy laden, and I will give you rest. Take my yoke upon you, and learn of me; for I am meek and lowly in heart: and ye shall find rest unto your souls. [Matt 11:28-29]"

Pride gives us the illusion that we are better than other people by our own strength or merit. This is offensive to God because it is He who has given us everything we currently hold.

"For who maketh thee to differ from another? and what has thou that thou didst not receive? Now if thou didst receive it, why dost thou glory, as if thou hadst not received it? [1 Cor 4:7]"

Let us be realistic. There are some people who are more talented and gifted than others. God does not contend with this fact. However, what God does contend with is when the more talented individual looks down pridefully upon the other less talented people as if he received the greater share of gifts by his owns hands or merit. Paul said he laboured more than all of the other apostles but it was not him but the grace of God which was upon him [1 Cor 15:10]. Remember the Pharisee who looked down upon the publican in the temple and thanked God that he was not like the other men, extortioners, unjust, adulterers and such the like? The Lord told us that the less talented publican went down to his house more justified than the publican: "for everyone that exalteth himself shall be abased; and he that humbleth himself shall be exalted [Lk 18:14]."

Some gifts and talents can be cultivated. But it is the grace of God which enables somebody to cultivate the gift in the first place. Therefore, glory must belong to God and God alone in everything. A prideful person takes the glory for himself and this makes him an enemy of truth. Not only does he look down upon other people, which is clearly not very kind, but he also robs God of the praise and glory which is due to His name. God is not well pleased with this behaviour.

Daniel and Nebuchadnezzar

When we are humble and appreciate that it is God who has given us all of the blessings which we possess then God will give us more of his abundance. But if we are prideful God will take away whatever we thought we gained by our own strength. This principle applies to everybody: both believer and unbeliever alike. And this is perfectly exemplified in two stories which involve both Daniel and Nebuchadnezzar.

The interesting observation about the two men is that one of them had very little but was very humble whilst the other man, who had a lot, and had received it all from the LORD, did not once deem it appropriate to attribute his glory and great wealth to God. Instead he took it upon himself to glory in his own strength.

I suppose this is nothing new:

"they spend their days in wealth, and in a moment go down to the grave. Therefore they say unto God, depart from us; for we desire not the knowledge of thy ways. What is the Almighty that we should serve him? and what profit should we have, if we pray unto him? [Job 21:13-15]."

Daniel was a servant when he attributed glory to God whereas Nebuchadnezzar was a mighty King when he gave glory to himself. Daniel was promoted because of his humility whereas Nebuchadnezzar was demoted because of his pride. When Daniel had interpreted Nebuchadnezzar's dream he gave all the glory to God. If anybody had a reason to be prideful then Daniel certainly did. Nebuchadnezzar had just had a terrible dream but when he awoke from his sleep he forgot it. He knew that it was a very important dream so he summoned all of his wise men, magicians and astrologers to recall the dream and to give him the interpretation thereof. The Chaldeans were open to giving him the interpretation but they were not too keen about the possibility of recalling his forgotten dream. They replied to the King that "there is not a man on earth who can tell the king's matter; therefore no king, lord, or ruler has ever asked such things of any magician, astrologer, or Chaldean. It is a difficult thing that the king requests, and there is no other who can tell it to the king except the gods, whose dwelling is not with flesh [Dan 2:10-11]." Nebuchadnezzar was wroth with the response and he issued a commandment to destroy all the wise men from the land of Babylon. This is when God used Daniel to step into the scene.

Daniel sought the LORD and he was confident God would answer his request. The man of God visited the King and asked him to give him some time to seek the face of the LORD. The King gave him some time so Daniel went back to his house and told the news to his co-labourers Hananiah, Mishael and Azariah. They cried out to the LORD and prayed, and that very same night God revealed the dream to Daniel in a night vision.

After receiving the dream and the interpretation thereof Daniel hasted to the courts of the King. The King was relieved when he saw his confidence. He optimistically asked Daniel whether he had been successful. Daniel replied "the secret which the king has demanded, the wise men, the astrologers, the magicians and the soothsayers cannot declare to the king. But there is a God in heaven who reveals secrets, and has made known to the King Nebuchadnezzar what will be in the latter days [Dan 2:27-28]."

Daniel gave glory to God straightway. What God had revealed to Daniel was impossible for man to understand or accomplish by his own intellect or strength. It was only possible through God, and Daniel understood this. God had revealed the dream to Nebuchadnezzar first but he intentionally made the king forget about it so that he might learn to depend upon God. If he had remembered the dream he would have probably glorified himself and said something along the lines of "how great a king I am that even the heavens and gods reveal vivid and prophetic dreams to me." God wanted to humble him so he made him forget the dream and rely upon another person for its recovery. He had to be dependent upon others and he later had to acknowledge that there was a God of gods, the Lord of the Hebrews, who had given him the dream and the interpretation thereof. God will do this to everybody at least once in their own respective lives. There will always be a day when we will be forced to rely upon the assistance of another person for progress. God does this so that we might learn that we ultimately need Him. But the great tragedy is that many still do not believe that they need the help of God. They continue to believe in self-sufficiency at the expense of the free and unbeatable assistance of the LORD. This is pride.

Daniel on the other hand gave praise to God because he was wise and understood how it was God who had worked the miracle and not himself. Whenever we are used to do the impossible we must remember to give praise to the LORD straightaway lest we fall into pride. Whether it be prophetic words, miracles, signs and healings, whatever supernatural deed we may perform, we must attribute all glory to the most High immediately. There are two reasons why we must do this.

Benefits of Humility

(1) When we glorify God people will turn to Him, repent and be saved. If we say that it is God who is the source of all love, knowledge and wisdom which we may possess, if we say that it is HE who is the motivating force behind all miracles, healings and other works of virtue which are performed by our hands, then people will be attracted to Him rather than us. As a result, they might be saved from their sins, for only He can save them.

King Nebuchadnezzar was so astounded after Daniel had given him the interpretation. He was so evidently surprised and relieved that he opted to even bow down and prostrate before the prophet.

But what he said to Daniel afterwards was more telling. "The King answered Daniel and said, Truly your God is the God of gods, the Lord of kings, and a revealer of secrets since you could reveal this secret [Dan 2:47]." Nebuchadnezzar gave praise to the living God because of Daniel's humility. Nebuchadnezzar had already bowed down and prostrated before Daniel. This shows us how he greatly respected and honoured the prophet. But when he opened his mouth he did not glorify or praise Daniel but he rightfully gave all the honour to God! If Daniel had not told the king about God, then the King would not have been open to the revelation of God and neither would he have praised his God. But because Daniel insisted upon God's assistance in the whole matter, Nebuchadnezzar was now given the opportunity to witness the work of God first hand. This was only made possible by Daniel's humility.

A similar episode is recounted in the Acts of the Apostles. After the day of Pentecost Peter and John went to the temple at Jerusalem to pray.

At the gate of the temple they encountered a lame man who was asking for alms. He had been lame from his mother's womb and he was well known to all those who acquainted themselves to the religious rites of the temple. The lame man did what he was used to doing. He requested for alms from the men who entered into the temple. But when he fixed his eyes upon Peter and John he received something extraordinary which he had not yet received before.

"Peter said, 'Look at us,' so he gave them his attention, expecting to receive something from them. Then Peter said, 'Silver and gold I do not have, but what I do have I give you: in the name of Jesus Christ of Nazareth, rise up and walk [Acts 3:4-6]."

Peter lifted the lame man up from his feet and his ankle bones received strength. He was immediately healed. "So he leaping up, stood and walked and entered the temple with them walking, leaping and praising God. And all the people saw him walking and praising God [Acts 3:8]."

When the lame man was healed many people rushed towards Peter and John. When Peter saw this he said to them "men of Israel, why do you marvel at this? Or why looks so intently at us, as though by our own power or godliness we had made this man walk? [Acts 3:12-13]" Peter gave the glory to God and used the miracle as an opportunity to preach to them about the resurrected Jesus. After hearing this sermon, we hear of how "many of those who heard the word believed; and the number of the men was about five thousand [Acts 4:4]."

The same principle was exhibited in the life of Jesus Christ. Jesus Christ never took the glory for himself but he always glorified God for whatever he managed to achieve. Jesus would always emphasise that he did nothing of himself: but that it was his Father dwelling upon him who would always do the good works through him. When he was approached by a man who called him good, Jesus quickly rebuffed the statement and clarified that none is good but God [Mk 10:30]. These are the marks of a humble man. Whenever Jesus performed a miracle or a healing he would always attribute it to God and thereby attract men to Him. When Jesus healed a man with palsy who was taken to him in a bed, he did not even lay hands upon him. He told him to arise and he did just that! The people who had witnessed this miracle were understandably shocked but they also glorified God for what they had just seen. They knew it had come from God because Jesus never spoke of himself but he always spoke of Him who sent him. "Now then the multitudes saw it, they marvelled and glorified God, who had given such power to men [Matt 9:8]."

The same thing happened when Jesus raised the son of the widow of Nain from the dead. "Then fear came upon all and they glorified God, saying 'a great prophet has risen up among us,' and 'God has visited his people." [Lk 7:10]

(2) The second benefit which we can receive from humility is promotion. Jesus makes this clear a number of times and the early Apostles in their letters emphasised this point too. Jesus told his disciples "whoever exalts himself will be humbled, and he who humbles himself will be exalted [Lk 14:11]."

Peter commanded the church to "humble yourselves under the mighty hand of God, that he may exalt you in due time [1 Pet 5:6]." This is a clear principle which must be learnt by all genuine believers. This principle of humility dictates that God exalts us when we humble ourselves. But when we exalt ourselves God will bring us down. The principle shows that there is a decision we make and a subsequent reaction which God brings about as a response. This is the concept of promotion. Promotion means to be exalted, to be lifted up higher in great esteem, honour and authority. God is telling the church that we will be promoted when we make all of our decisions from a place of humility. This is what happened to the Lord Jesus Christ in his life. Paul recounts how he "humbled himself and became obedient to the point of death, even the death of the cross [Phi 2:8]." As a result, "God also has highly exalted him and given him the name which is above every name that at the name of Jesus every knee should bow, of those in heaven, and of those on earth, and of those under the earth [Phi 2:9-10]."

Humility is dependent upon obedience. If you find somebody who is obedient to the word of God, then he will inevitably be humble. Paul says "he humbled himself and became obedient to the point of death." This shows us that there is a clear relationship between obedience and humility. The obedience which Jesus Christ showed was perfect. He obeyed the Father even during difficult and shameful circumstances. Dying on a cross was a shameful punishment for a man who did no wrong. We must also remember that they mocked him scourged him, spat on him, pulled his beard and did all manner of other unwarranted deeds to him. And amidst all of this he did not speak a bad word back to them. In fact, he prayed for them and continued to keep his silence. Jesus obeyed the word of God amidst all of this. He exhibited perfect humility even when he could not quite understand the extremity of his affliction.

Jesus Christ was promoted for his obedience to God. The humility which was in him was provided by the Spirit of God. It was not a false humility but a humility which arose from the nature of God. Remember Jesus Christ said "I and my Father are one [Jn 10:30]." But before he said this he also acknowledged that the Father is greater than all [Jn 10:29]. This statement was an acknowledgment of truth, not false humility. For God is clearly greater than all. He counts the strands of hairs upon each man and he calls the stars by their names. He split the Red Sea with the breath of his nostrils and he spoke all of creation into existence with the sound of his word. Who is like unto Him amongst the gods? Nobody. I know not one. But an awareness of this fact is not false humility at all but a simple acknowledgement of the truth. Jesus knew this and yet he was able to say that "I and my Father are one." This is because God abode within Jesus. This shows us that God is humble. He is humble enough to lower himself into an atmosphere where he was loathed and despised for his righteousness. The light lowered himself into the darkness and the darkness did not comprehend the light nor love it. God knew he would be rejected by the majority and yet he humbled himself into the vessel of a man and took the punishment of sins which all mankind rightfully deserved. This shows us that the source of pure humility resides in God and not in us. Meekness and humility is the fruit of the Spirit. And man is naturally prideful and hostile to the ways of God. But our humility can be made perfect when God dwells within us. We must show humility in the first place to obey God and submit to him. But even this act of obedience comes as a result of the goodness and grace of God. When we do submit to God and obey Him diligently the Spirit of God will now work through us—as it did in the case of Jesus Christ—to shape us in perfect humility.

Humility is the acknowledgment of truth. It is the awareness that we are nothing without the grace of God. If it was not for the grace of God none of us would receive the Spirit of God and the gifts which are accompanied with him. This is grace. But it is humility which enables us to understand this and apply it. The way we apply it is two-fold: firstly, it determines our interactions with other people and secondly our relationship with God. With other people we will never believe that we are above them or better than them. In fact, we will think the opposite and actually consider them to be above us. This is what the Apostle Paul thought. He said he was the least of the apostles, "who am not worthy to be called an apostle, because I persecuted the church of God [1 Cor 15:9]." And yet he conceded how he laboured more than all of the other apostles because of the grace of God abounded upon him greatly. Paul genuinely believed he was the worst of all sinners. He repeated this conviction in his first epistle to Timothy.

"This is a faithful saying and worthy of all acceptance, Jesus came into the world to save sinners, of whom I am chief. However for this reason I obtained mercy, that in me first Jesus Christ might show all longsuffering, as a pattern to those are going to believe on him for everlasting life [1 Tim 1:15-16]."

Paul understood that he was the chief of all sinners but he gave thanks to God for the grace which transformed him into the holy and mighty man he later became. Paul was a very talented man. But Paul understood how all of his talents were given to him by God and not through any merit of his own. If anybody deserved the talents he received it should not have been him because he was actually one of the worst sinners prior to his adoption. And yet God chose him, and equipped him with so much grace and glory, in order to showcase to the world the great depths and riches of His mercy and grace.

This understanding which Paul received enabled him to keep humble in front of his brethren. He often recalled in his mind his early days of rebellion and this kept him rooted in the humility of Christ. It is helpful for us to remember what Christ has brought us through and how he has transformed us. This will keep us humble in front of all people. For example, sometimes I have found myself mocking or deriding pagans and polytheists. Then the Holy Spirit reminds me how I once held views which were sympathetic with paganism for a short period of my life. This remembrance keeps me lowly and thankful for God's grace. It is this acknowledgment of my past which enables me to understand how "by the grace of God I am what I am [1 Cor 15:10]."

The second part of our humility is about our interaction with God. This deals with our understanding of how we approach God. It deals with self-righteousness and our own bankruptcy in comparison to God's grace. Humans have the tendency to believe they are good before a holy and infallible God. This is a mistake because nobody can come even close to the perfection of God. Isaiah understood this when he had a magnificent vision of the Lord high and lifted up on his throne in the heavenly temple. Isaiah said "woe is me" because he received the revelation that none of his works of righteousness could appease the holy God. Isaiah begun his prophetic ministry before he saw the vision of Jesus Christ. So he was peculiarly righteous in a midst of a rebellious nation. This would have likely resulted in some form of self-righteousness on his part. But when he finally saw the splendour of God's holiness he was too afraid to even look upon Him or approach Him; and he understood there and then how all of his righteousness which he had relied upon before was akin to an unclean, filthy thing before God.

Isaiah received God's grace. One of the seraphim flew to the prophet and touched his mouth with a coal which had been taken from the altar. Then the seraph told the prophet that his iniquity had been taken away from him and that his sin had now been purged [Isa 6:7]. Isaiah's iniquity was purged not by his own works but by God's grace. It was God's seraph and God's coal which He had given to the prophet to cleanse him. It was God's goodness which lead to Isaiah's repentance. After this encounter Isaiah certainly walked with God in humility. We know this because God had told him:

"thus says the High and lofty One who inhabits eternity, whose name is holy: 'I dwell in the high and holy place, with him also who has a contrite and humble spirit, to revive the spirit of the humble and to revive the heart of the contrite ones [Isa 57:15]."

The same applies to us today. We are only allowed to enter into his presence by the means of the blood which was shed for us by his Son on the cross. This fact should dissolve any suspicions of self-righteousness which may arise within our hearts. We can only approach God in the Holy of holies by the blood of Jesus and not by our own works of self-righteousness. This acknowledgement should keep us humble and keep us indebted, forever thankful, to the grace of God which has prevailed in our lives and has set us free from the bondage of our sins. If we are self-righteous—i.e we believe we can approach God because of our own good works—then we are certainly acting out of a place of pride. Paul lets us know in the epistle to the Romans that Abraham may have had a reason to glory in front of his neighbours for the great works he achieved in their sight. However, none of these works could warrant glory from God. It was his faith which pleased God, not necessarily his works which were outside of the influence of his faith [Rom 4:1-3].

The same principle applies to us today. We only please God when we have faith in his Word and act upon it. God provides the sacrifice, the grace and the righteousness, and God only expects faith on our part in return. God's way of sacrifice, so that we might receive remission for our sins and atonement, is the only way to please Him and we cannot imagine that we have another way better. When Adam and Eve sinned they sowed a garment of fig leaves. But God replaced these with a garment of animal skins. When Cain took his sacrifice to God the Lord rejected it in place of Abel's sacrifice which was accepted by the Lord and prescribed by Him. This shows us that there is a way which seems right to men but these ways do not necessarily please God. Self-righteousness is a way which seems right to men but later results in destruction. God is the source of our righteousness so we must go to him in faith to receive it. This awareness should keep us humble in the midst of a holy and magnificent God.

When Daniel interpreted Nebuchadnezzar's dream he was subsequently promoted. Daniel was promoted despite the fact he gave glory to God for what he was able to do. The same thing happened in the life of Joseph. God enabled Joseph to interpret the dream of Pharaoh and when Joseph caught the attention of the Egyptian King, Joseph gave all glory to God. Both Joseph and Daniel were promoted for their humility. These are two clear old Testament examples which illustrate the principle of promotion.

When Daniel was promoted he petitioned the king to set Shadrach, Meschach and Abednego over the affairs of the province of Babylon. The King hearkened unto Daniel and the other men of God were promoted too. This means other people can benefit from our humility. If we are humble before God and remain so it will only be a matter of time before we are promoted by God in whatever sphere of life we inhabit. When God blesses us for our humility we will now be empowered to bless other children of God around us.

Pride Results in Demotion

But the principle of promotion has a reverse effect called the principle of demotion. This dictates that pride can result in demotion in much the same way that humility before God will always result in promotion. Nebuchadnezzar is a perfect example of somebody who was temporarily demoted because of his pride. In the book of Daniel the author recounts how the King of Babylon one day found himself gloating over the splendour of his kingdom. As he was walking around his royal palace he began to say within himself "Is not this great Babylon, that I have built for a royal dwelling by the might power and for the honour of my majesty? [Dan 4:30]"

As he was saying this he heard a voice from heaven which began to decree judgment against him. He was told that the kingdom was to depart from him and that he would be driven into the wilderness to dwell with the beasts of the field. He would eat grass like the oxen and would continue to do so until he understood that it was God who is in control of all the kingdoms of men. The word was fulfilled immediately and that very same hour Nebuchadnezzar was driven into the wilderness. And there he remained—where his hair had grown like eagle feathers and his nails like bird's claws—until he lifted up his eyes into heaven and acknowledged God.

Nebuchadnezzar testified in the immediate aftermath how "my understanding returned to me" [Dan 4:34].

When we are prideful we lose our basic understanding of how it is God who is at the helm of all affairs, powers and blessings. Nebuchadnezzar looked into the heavens when he received his understanding back. Perhaps he looked at the celestial bodies, perhaps the sun or the moon and the stars, and realised how it wasn't he who was responsible for their splendour, but God alone. He had amassed great wealth, power and dominion on the earth but there still remained an even greater splendour, order and power in the heavens, which was there by no means of his own hands. When he saw this he thought of God. And he blessed the most High and praised him for his unsearchable glory. Nebuchadnezzar recounts how "at the same time my reason returned to me [Dan 4:36]." The king had his dominion and honour restored to him. He was finally able to conclude with these wise words: "those who walk in pride He is able to put down [Dan 4:37]."

Indeed this has been the case since the beginning of mankind. Early on in the history of mankind, shortly after the great flood, there arose a great civilization which sought to assert and exalt itself above the stars of heaven. This kingdom was founded in Babel and it was led by the great hunter and king called Nimrod. The people of this land had been constructing a tower. And they said "come let us build ourselves a city, and a tower whose top is in the heavens; let us make a name for ourselves, lest we be scattered abroad over the face of the whole earth [Gen 11:4]."

God had commanded the descendants of Noah to spread across the four corners of the earth. But they disobeyed Him and thought otherwise. There is a great connection between disobedience and pride and it is exhibited by all those who disobey the word of God. The inhabitants thought they could govern their own lives better than God. So they sought to make a name for themselves—a name at enmity with the name of God—and in the vanity of their own minds they began to imagine waging war against God. Their plans were quickly scuppered. The LORD confused the uniformity of their language and scattered them across the face of the earth. These men and women who had exalted themselves before the face of God were quickly diminished and abased. Does this not happen to all who lift up their hands against the Lord in pride?

"Why do the heathen rage, and the people imagine a vain thing?

The kings of the earth set themselves, and the rulers take counsel together, against the LORD, and against his anointed, saying,

Let us break their bands asunder, and cast away their cords from us.

He that sitteth in the heavens shall laugh: the Lord shall have them in derision.

Then shall he speak unto them in his wrath, and vex them in his sore displeasure. [Psa 2:1-5]"

The same thing is spoken of by Isaiah regarding Lucifer. Lucifer said in his heart, "I will ascend into heaven. I will exalt my throne above the stars of God . . . I will ascend above the heights of the clouds, I will be like the most High [Isa 14:12-14]." Lucifer was told he would be brought down to Sheol, "to the lowest depths of the pit [Isa 14:15]." The same destiny is surely promised to anybody who follows after Lucifer's footsteps.

When we receive power, the blessings of God and prosperity, the trouble is that we may grow prideful, forgetting that it was God who was the source of all our riches and success. God will reward us when we are faithful. But when he rewards us we must remember Him and continue to walk in humility before the presence of His throne. The 12 disciples were greatly rewarded by God for following Jesus. But then they began to contest amongst themselves as to who was the greatest. John and James sought to sit beside the Lord Jesus after the resurrection from the dead, one to the right and the other on the left. They had already begun exalting themselves in their hearts. But Jesus corrected them. He told them that this was the way of the world: whereby the rulers of the gentiles would exalt themselves above their subjects. Jesus told them that rulership in the kingdom of God operated under different principles. The greatest would have to lower himself to become the lowest. He would have to take the place of a humble servant to excel. This is the way of the cross and this is the way the Lord Jesus invites all of his saints to humbly embrace.

"And what does the LORD require of you but to do justly, to love mercy, and to walk humbly with your God? [Mic 6:8]"

When we are humble we do not focus upon ourselves but rather upon God and Him alone. This is why Moses did not know that his face shone like the sun after coming down from Mount Horeb. He was so fixed on the face of God, and not his own glory. This results in great humility because the more we look at God instead of ourselves then the more we come to realise how small we are in comparison to his profoundly massive glory.

KEYS TO HUMILITY

Let us recap some of the keys we alluded to before. They will help us remain humble before God and man; and they will thereby result in our promotion in every area of our lives.

1. Remember the grace of God. Forget and deny your own self-righteousness and remember that your holiness comes through faith in the death and resurrection of the Lord Jesus. Remember that it is his blood, and not your own works and righteousness, which enables you to come boldly before the presence of the Father. Give thanks to the LORD for what he has done through sending his Son onto the earth for us.
2. Remember that every spiritual gift we have received was given to us freely by the grace of God. Remember that it was given to serve the body of Christ and now yourself. There are two good ways for us to remember this. Firstly, we should stay renewed in the word of God. Secondly we should develop a spirit of thankfulness.
3. Fasting is a great way of remaining humble. David said "But as for me, when they were sick, my clothing *was* sackcloth: I humbled my soul with fasting; and my prayer returned into mine own bosom."
4. Build relationships with people who are more gifted and successful than yourself.
5. Learn how to lead through service.
6. Think of all people as being better than yourself.
7. Recall to mind the sinner you were before Jesus saved you.
8. Seek counsel and obey it when it is in line with the Word of God.
9. Read and obey God's commandments.

Focus

Focus is defined as the main or central point of something, the ability to remain attentive towards a particular point of interest. Focus is one of the most important qualities which a saint requires in order to walk successfully with God. Without focus God will be very far. Although God is very close to all of us we will never know this until we actually focus upon his presence and his person.

Focus is important for anybody who wants to be successful. Ask anybody who excels in whatever discipline they have chosen, say business, basketball, art or music. If you were to ask them what was instrumental in their accomplishments two virtues would immediately spring to mind. They would immediately highlight focus and passion. These two virtues are interconnected: for if I am passionate towards something then I will certainly remain focused on it and if I am focused upon something then this would imply that I am passionate towards it.

Focus is so important in a world where there are so many distractions. If we do not remain focused, then we will not be able to achieve much. In a world where there are countless distractions, social media, sports, and vain television programmes to name a few, relationships which do not contribute or edify us towards God's plan for our lives, a plethora of pointless activities and distractions which do not gear us towards our destiny in this life, we must be sure to continually renew our minds daily with the word of God to remind us that we are called to be about the Father's business.

The first thing we must do before we remain focused is to identify what we must be focused upon. In other words we must have a clear vision. If I wanted to study at Harvard Law School this would be my vision. But I would now need to remain focused to prepare if I wanted to succeed. Personally I cannot recall a time when I was successful in any pursuit without first focusing. Anytime I have coveted after something, and I have not been successful, then this was simply because I was not focused enough. I am sure the same has applied for you in your life too. When it came to entering into university, gaining a place in a youth drama school, securing a job I desperately desired—whatever I have successfully pursued in my life so far—in all instances highlighted I only found myself being successful because of my focus.

My focus resulted in two things. Firstly I minimised all distractions and procrastination. This resulted in hard-work. And secondly I continued to meditate and continually think upon the vision. Whenever we do this we will surely be successful in whatever we pursue. This is a principle of life: for focus guarantees success. This is a principle which is clearly important for our pursuit of God too. If our vision is to know God and we focus upon this with all of our heart then we will surely find Him. This is why God inspired the prophet Jeremiah to say that "ye shall seek me, and find me, when ye shall search for me with all your heart [Jer 29:13]." Focus implies being wholehearted. When we are focused we pursue our vision with everything that is inside of us; not half of our heart or most of it, but with all of it. This is why David testifies "blessed are they . . . that seek Him with the whole heart [Psa 119:2]." When we seek and focus upon God with the whole heart then we will find Him, who is the source of all good things and blessings; for God is a God who rewards those who diligently seek Him [Heb 11:6].

Focus of Jesus

Jesus' ministry was short but very successful. This was made possible because of his unwavering focus. Jesus knew the vision which God had impressed within his soul and he did everything to ensure that it was manifested sooner rather than later. It is wise for us to first focus on what God is calling us to do on this earth. We must ask him questions about our destiny scroll. After we have done this we must now focus on fulfilling everything God has created us to do. If we do this, we will have great success and accomplish our overall mandate. This is what the Lord Jesus did.

In a prayer the Lord made to the Father before his betrayal, he said "I have glorified thee on the earth: I have finished the work which thou gavest me to do [Jn 17:4]." God gave Jesus the vision and the work he had to do. But Jesus had to focus upon accomplishing the vision in order to succeed and fulfil the plan which God had ordained for him. Jesus was clearly successful in doing this.

When we look at some of the statements Jesus made during his ministry it becomes evidently clear that the Lord was an extremely focused man who gave his all to fulfil his Father's vision. This is why he was able to fulfil so many prophecies which were spoken about him by the prophets of old in only three and a half years! He knew what God had called him to do and he remained focused every single day, every single moment, until he was finally crucified upon the cross. He yielded every thought and desire under the Father's will and he thereby remained focused throughout his whole ministry. He continued to meditate upon the commandments of God and the vision God had sent him, and he was thereby empowered to operate in the strength of the Holy Ghost. Because of his infallible focus he remained immune to any of the temptations which were offered by the Devil. Even when he was young at the age of twelve years old he startled his parents when he revealed his diligent focus to them: "How is it that ye sought me? wist ye not that I must be about my Father's business? [Lk 2:49]" said Jesus to them as they found him in the Temple hearing and asking the doctors questions. He was focused preparing for his life purpose from such a young age.

When we are focused we will avoid procrastination at all costs. Procrastination is the act of delaying or postponing something, it is when we promise we will accomplish something tomorrow when it is within our means to do it today. Jesus did not procrastinate. Jesus had a routine of seeking the Father daily, particularly in the morning, discovering what the will of the Father was for that day, and then he would work tirelessly accomplishing it under the unction and guidance of the Holy Ghost during the remainder of the day.

It is one thing to know the overall vision and will of God for our lives but it is another thing to discern daily what God wants us to do in order to maximise our potential and gifts upon the earth. For instance, we may know that God has called us to be holy and without blemish before Him in love. We may also know that God has called us to be conformed into the image of his Son and to cast out demons, heal the sick and cleanse the lepers, yes, this is His purpose and vision for all of us in this life. But what is God calling us to do on a daily basis before we reach this perfect stature? Jesus knew the long-term vision which God had called him to accomplish but he was also aware of the daily targets God had ordained for him to fulfil. This is why Jesus was so focused. He delighted in doing the will of the Father and he had a clear vision of what God had called him to do everyday. Jesus earnestly sought the will of the Father. He then ensured he was vigilantly focused to fulfil it.

This is what Jesus said: "I must work the works of him that sent me, while it is day: the night cometh, when no man can work [Jn 9:4]."

Procrastination is not a wise position to remain in. I say 'remain in' because procrastination is a habit we can stay trapped in unless we actively combat it daily and choose to become aggressively focused. The virtue of focus is a habit we must develop. Jesus had already learnt the virtue of focus before he began his ministry at 30, he did not become focused overnight. The Holy Spirit empowered him to be supernaturally focused, even during times when his flesh wanted to give up. But he still worked on his focus before he received the anointing from God. Becoming focused was a life choice which Jesus choose to develop even before he began his ministry.

Jesus said he had to work during the day before the night came [Jn 9:4] because he understood there was a time limit under which he could accomplish the vision. All men die at some stage and tomorrow is not promised for anybody. This is why we must remain focused today and abstain from any form of procrastination. It is so easy for us to say I will become holy and live a righteous life next year or when I am older - I have heard this a number of times from the younger generation when I evangelise to them. But how is tomorrow promised to anybody? Jesus said in a parable he would come as a thief in the night, in an unexpected hour when some of his servants were drinking and eating with the drunken and smiting their fellowservants [Matt 24:49]. I am sure that these are the believers who are not focused, they are the servants who have continually procrastinated and said in their hearts that they will become righteous when they are older.

Seasons of Focus During Examinations

I can remember two particular seasons in my life which preceded two important examinations. One of them was before entering into university when I completed the International Baccalaureate and the other was in my final year at university before I received my degree. When I was at sixth form I received an offer to study at my dream choice, the University of Oxford, to study my dream course Philosophy Politics and Economics. I had been given an offer and I had to fulfil the conditions of the offer before I could enter in. This is called a conditional offer and I had received it a few days before Christmas with just over five months before my final school exams. My vision was clear—to ensure I fulfilled the conditions of my offer, and now I was given a five month target to remain focused. I was very determined and I remained focused throughout this whole time-span. When the exams began in May I was adequately prepared and confident. I was understandably nervous but I thank God I managed to exceed my expectations!

When I look back now I know fully well why I was successful. (1) I was very focused. (2) I managed to leave ample time to prepare before the exams.

These two conditions were certainly exercised in the life of Jesus Christ. He was always focused upon the will of the Father and he was preparing for his ministry from at least 12 years of age. We must be truthful here. It is impossible for us to succeed in anything in life unless we leave enough preparation time to stay focused. Ask any successful boxer or athlete. Have any become a champion by procrastinating and insufficiently preparing? Paul said the athletes of his day were temperate and focused as they prepared for the games. They did this for a corruptible crown and yet we are told to strive for an incorruptible crown [1 Cor 9:25]. We cannot wait until we become focused but we must learn to become focused today! This is something I learnt in my last year of university before I sat my final exams.

I was very lazy during my time at university. I did not have a clear vision of what I wanted to achieve, or what I wanted to do after university, so I often procrastinated and pursued after other things which were offered to me in the campus, such as smoking, drinking and finding women. The truth is that everybody is focused upon something. But some of us are focused upon dangerous and profitless pursuits whilst others are focused upon meaningful and profitable pursuits. I was focused upon revelry and debauchery when I should have been focused upon doing well in my exams. As a result, I only began revising for the exams a month before I sat them and much of my revision was focused upon catching up on work I did not cover over the course of my two prior years. I left so much to do at the end and unsurprisingly I did not do too well. Despite passing the exams I knew I could have done so much better had I remained focused throughout the whole year.

This has taught me about something in the body of Christ. Some of us will 'pass' the examination of our salvation but we will not do as well as we ought to have done. This will be because of procrastination, lack of focus and inadequate preparation. Think of the life of Samson, the Nazarite from birth and the mighty man of valour. This man was gifted with extraordinary supernatural strength. He was also gifted with wisdom and yet he failed to fulfil his potential because of the lack of focus which was exhibited in his life. He focused on women when he should have been focusing upon his people who he was chosen to judge and lead. Alas! his ministry was cut prematurely short when he was betrayed by Delilah the woman who he had fallen in love with. And his eyes, symbolic for the vision he had now lost as a result, were now cut off to serve as a reminder and lesson for all the children of God who fail to remain focused. Now it is unreasonable to suggest that Samson was sent to hell for his mistake, although he had fallen for the same mistake quite a few times in his life. Nevertheless, we can safely conclude that he was unable to maximise the potential which was implanted into him upon earth. The same thing will happen to us if we do not remain focused upon our vision to walk with God. Focus in the kingdom of God will require us to cut back all forms of distractions which ultimately get in the way from enabling us to remain focused on our one most important desire: intimacy with Jesus Christ.

Another important principle I learnt during my time at university is to remain focused on one thing and only one thing at a time. In other words, I found that it was impossible to stay focused upon two things, especially if they were at odds with each other at the same time. Most of my time at university was focused upon smoking, drinking, generally enjoying the lusts of my flesh and chasing women. But when the time for my examinations dawned upon the horizon I found it difficult to shift my focus towards academic pursuits. I had to stop focusing upon enjoying myself with my social life because this lifestyle was incompatible with the demand of long hours of study and revision. The two lifestyles were incompatible and because it took me some time to overcome my past focus of revelry and to develop the new focus of diligent study, I suffered as a result.

The same observation can be made for the things of God. If I look into the world then I cannot look at God. And if I focus upon the things which are found in the world then I cannot focus upon the things which are of God. A double minded man is not only unstable in all of his ways but he is also unproductive and unsuccessful. I have learnt and understood this not only in my secular life but also with my walk with God. Jesus said you are either for me or against me; he said that he that gathers not with him scatters abroad [Matt 12:30]. Jesus is basically saying that we either focus upon him or we do not. If we do not focus upon him then we are against him and if we do not gather our attention and all of our faculties to focus upon him then we scatter his grace and anointing. This is a common principle which can be found in any pursuit. Those who focus upon one thing are more likely to be successful than those who focus on two contrary pursuits.

This is why Jesus says no man can serve two masters [Matt 6:24]. This is true, especially when we consider two masters which are contrary to one another. Jesus notes that God and mammon are two masters which are at enmity with one another, but another two which are at enmity with one another are the Spirit and the flesh. "For the flesh lusts against the Spirit and the Spirit against the flesh: and these are contrary the one to the other: so that you cannot do the things you would [Gal 5:17]."

This is why the Lord Jesus exhorts his disciples to have a single eye. A single eye is one which is focused and irremovably fixed on one position. It only looks at one thing. It only has one desire. It only has one pursuit.

A single eye is in reference to the inner eye, the eye of the soul which compromises the intellect, will and emotions. This is what Paul meant when he said whatsoever you do in word or deed, let all be done in the name of the Lord Jesus [Col 3:17]. This is also what the Lord meant when he said continue to seek the Kingdom of God and his righteousness and then all other things will be added to you. To have a single eye denotes an unwavering and committed focus upon the things of God and the things of God alone at every moment of the day.

In the case of Jesus his eye was unquestionably looking towards God. Jesus was always focused upon communing with God and drawing closer to Him. Jesus loved the Father and always sought to do His will. The Lord did not focus on God because it was a mere religious duty or ritual but he focused upon the Father because he loved Him and sought to be intimate with Him at every given opportunity. This is the same reason why we must do the same, not because we desire any earthly gain from Him in return, but simply because we love Him.

When Jesus says 'let your eye be single' what he is really commanding his disciples to do is to seek God as an end in himself. Jesus tells us to do this because we love Him and desire His presence as a meaningful and valuable end in itself. He is not saying let your eye be single so that God may give you glamour, riches and worldly rewards in return but he is saying seek God with a single eye so that your reward might be God and God alone.[1]

If there is any other reason why we seek God, then our eye is not

---

[1] As we do this then God will give us more specific instructions about what He has created us to accomplish and how he expects us to fulfil our own specific calling in our lives. I have found that God can do this with you alone (through dreams, through visions or even through his still small voice) but he can also send you people who will give you prophetic words which confirm and encourage you with an idea of what your specific mission is during this life.

single but it is what Jesus would call an evil-eye. Jesus says that the light of the body is the eye: and if our eye is single then our body will be full of light. But Jesus goes onto say that if it our eye is evil then our body will be full of darkness. The light which Jesus speaks of is symbolic for righteousness and enlightenment. When our focus is upon God and Him alone then God will impart us with all wisdom, knowledge, righteousness and enlightenment. This is the whole cusp of the gospel: not that we are made wise or righteous by any works which we have done by our self, but by the grace we receive when we continue to look upon Jesus who is the finisher and author of our salvation. In him dwells all the riches of wisdom and knowledge. And in him dwells the fullness of light and righteousness. So we are transformed "into the same image from glory to glory, even as by the Spirit of the Lord [2 Cor 3:18]" when we remain focused upon his Being and fixated upon his presence.

One of the major concerns about focusing upon God and His Christ is the problem of conceptualisation. We may find it difficult to focus and visualise something which is invisible to us. This is a problem I used to have. But I have now overcome it by experience and practise. The first thing I seek for when I focus upon God is clarity and peace. When I have these two things then I know that the presence of God is around me and that I have managed to focus upon God adequately. Remember God is not the author of confusion, anxiety or fear, so when we have these problems clouding our minds then we can be certain that we are failing to exercise our ability to keep our eye single. I am not saying that we will nor endure these problems momentarily, we certainly will for they are often the results of spiritual encroachments, but when we are focused upon God consistently we should rarely face these problems. This is how I am able to discern whether I am focusing upon God sufficiently or not.

"Thou wilt keep him in perfect peace, whose mind is stayed on thee: because he trusteth in thee [Isa 26:3]."

I also like to focus upon His throne room too in order to help visualise his presence and Being. In the Book of Hebrews the Holy Ghost informs us that the LORD reigns on mount Sion with an innumerable host of angels. In other prophetic books such as the book of Isaiah and the book of Revelation the prophets give us a greater glimpse of the immediate surroundings around God's throne. Jesus Christ is seated on the right hand of the throne and before him are the Seraphim, Cherubim and the 24 Elders. When I am worshipping and praising the LORD sometimes I visualise this to help my focus.

When we look at the context under which Jesus said 'let thine eye be single' we are able to gain a clearer picture of what he meant. Before Jesus made this statement he was telling his disciples not to focus upon the treasures of the world, which are but temporary, but to focus upon the treasures which are eternal. He then told his disciples "where your treasure is there will your heart be also". The heart is often used synonymously with the soul. The soul contains the faculties of the intellect, mind, emotions and will. Jesus was trying to shift and transform the earthly mind-set of his disciples. He was instructing them: do not focus upon those things which are temporary but focus upon those treasures which are of eternal value. He was telling them how it was difficult, if not impossible, to focus upon two contrary pursuits. He was exhorting them to be of one mind—i.e to have a single eye—in order to minimise all distractions and thereby maximise all focus upon the kingdom of God.

Jesus reemphasises this point in a couple of parables. He tells his disciples that the kingdom of heaven is like a treasure which is hid in a field. A man later finds the treasure in the field and he is joyful at the discovery. After doing so he decides to sell all that he has and buy the field. He disposes all of his old possessions and now focuses upon the cultivation of the field. Jesus communicates the same principle in another parable. In the parable of the merchant man he describes the kingdom of heaven as a merchant man who seeks goodly pearls: "who when he had found one pearl of great price went and sold all that he had and bought it [Mk 13:45-46]." Jesus uses businessmen in both of these parables to address the concepts of diversification and specialisation. Diversification is a business term which denotes the process of a company enlarging and varying its range of products for profit; whereas specialisation on the other hand is the process of concentrating on and becoming an expert in one particular subject or skill. In these parables we find two men who choose to specialise in the treasure of God. They were seeking a treasure of real value and then they found God. After doing so they both sold all that they previously possessed and choose to focus upon God alone.

In the first parable Jesus says the man even 'hides' in the field. [This may remind of us of John the Baptists mother who when she conceived of the boy hide herself five months [Lk 1:24]]. He is not willing to let anything distract him on his walk with God and he has chosen to 'sell'—which is to dispose of—all things which are now meaningless to him.

The concept of specialisation and diversification teaches us that we can become an expert in one field when we choose to specialise rather than diversify. A teacher who specialises in Geography will attain a much richer understanding in this one subject if he specialises in it alone than if he decides to study all of the subjects in humanities such as history and religion. This is something which is applicable to us when we choose to devote all of our faculties to focus upon the things of God. If we devote all of our attention to the kingdom of God and do not divide our focus upon the things of the world, we will specialise much more on the nature of God than we could ever possibly achieve with a double mind.

"If ye then be risen with Christ, seek those things which are above, where Christ sitteth on the right hand of God. Set your affection on things above, not on things on earth [Col 3:1-2]."

Jesus wants us to be focused on his righteousness which is imputed unto us through faith. When we focus on his righteousness we are filled with the necessary Christ-like virtues such as love, gentleness, compassion and meekness which are all necessary for us to exhibit the nature of God. God calls us to seek the kingdom and God and his righteousness and then promises us to receive other good things as a result. This is true and we will find that as we focus on this God will teach and instruct us with other important, practical areas which are needed for us to develop in this life. He will teach us about the importance of being excellent, trustworthy, loyal and humble in our workplace; he will teach us about the importance of maintaining healthy relationships with our families and our friends; he will teach us about the importance of being generous and helpful to those around us; and there will be a number of other specific assignments—which will differ in all of our lives—which God will give us as we walk with a single eye of righteousness and love. Some may be called into Business, others into education or the work of full-time ministry, whatever it is that God is calling you into, I believe it will only become clear when you walk with a single eye of focus towards the Kingdom of God and his righteousness.

Mary of Bethany

In the gospel of Luke, we are introduced to two sisters called Mary and Martha. We are told that Mary sat at Jesus' feet and heard his word whilst Martha her sister was distracted with much serving. Martha was not pleased that her sister was unhelpful and she lodged her complaint to the Lord Jesus.

"And Jesus answered and said unto her, Martha, Martha, thou art careful and troubled about many things: but one thing is needful: and Mary hath chosen that good part, which shall not be taken away from her [Lk 10:41-42]."

One of the best ways we can cultivate the skill of focus is by learning how to listen. Many of us have poor focus because we have not learned to exercise the art of listening. Mary of Bethany's listening skills were exemplary: when Martha began to complain to the Lord about her lack of assistance Mary did not even respond but she continued to listen and focus upon Jesus' word. It is important that we learn to focus whenever we listen to God's word and read it. It is easy for us to let our mind wander when we are reading the Bible or listening to the word of God. But if Mary can achieve success when it comes to focus then so can we. We just need to develop a heart-felt and intense intimacy with the Lord Jesus. We do this by learning how to listen to him.

Focus is something that will make you seem strange to the outside world and not everybody will be able to understand you. Mary of Bethany was extremely focused when it came to pleasing Christ and drawing intimately towards him, but many people including her sister could not understand her. When Mary broke an alabaster box and poured the perfume on Jesus' feet to anoint him, the disciples were confused and agitated. Judas objected to her display of devotion and asked the

Lord whether such a move could have been profitable when the money could have been used to feed the poor [Jn 12:3-5].

Jesus defended her and told his disciples that she would always be remembered for her abundant generosity. This shows us how the enemy will always try to make you doubt whether focusing upon God is of any value. The enemy will often ask you, especially in times of discord and distress, "what is the Almighty, that we should serve him? and what profit should we have, if we pray unto him? [Job 21:15]." The enemy is a liar and he knows our strength lies within our ability to remain irremovably focused upon Jesus Christ the chief cornerstone. Mary was told that her name would be told for memorial wherever the gospel was preached all over the earth [Matt 26:13], in other words that she would have a very long-lasting legacy for her devotion to Christ. So we should never believe our focus on Christ will be in vain.

Moses was a man of God who focused ardently upon the presence of God and he left a great legacy as a result. Moses face shone like the Sun because his focus upon the LORD was so irremovable that nobody could take his eyes off Him. Moses would often ascend upon the top of the holy mount to focus upon God alone and to remove all distractions from the world below. The scriptures testify that "there arose not a prophet since in Israel like unto Moses, whom the LORD knew face to face [Deu 34:10]." Moses received this legacy because his face was always set towards the face of God. God's face is always set towards the earth but very rarely does He find a face which is set towards His.

If we want to live a life of focus, we need to walk with other people who are like-minded. We cannot walk this life alone so we must be very wise in choosing the people we want to walk with in this path of life. Solomon observed how

"two are better than one because they have a good reward for their labour. For if they fall, the one will lift up his fellow; but woe to him that is alone when he falleth; for he hath not another to help him up. Again, if two lie together, then they have heat: but how can one be warm alone? [Ecc 4:9-11]"

It is not good that man should be alone [Gen 2:18]. Man must build relationships with others even as the Lord sought to build relationships with his twelve disciples. But he must choose wisely with those who he decides to invest his time with. Mary the mother of Jesus decided to spend three months with Elizabeth the mother of John the Baptist because they were like-minded. If Mary had told her family and friends about the Son she had divinely received from the LORD, then everybody around her would have surely thought she was either mad or lying. Even Joseph her fiancé was going to put her away until he was visited in a dream by the angel of the LORD who comforted and informed him of the divinity of Mary's son. But Mary had to spend time with somebody who would understand her and help her to remain focused with her vision. This person was Elizabeth, and during this time they helped one another to remain focused on the supernatural plan which God ordained for each of their lives.

Jesus on Focus

When we are so focused upon the pursuit of a particular goal we will even offset and deny basic necessities in order to achieve the vision at hand. This is what Jesus often did when he fasted for extended periods of time. When his disciples once brought him some food to eat he denied the offer saying "my meat is to do the will of him that sent me, and to finish his work [Jn 4:34]." There are some basic requirements which our flesh will naturally desire. Among these will include food, water, sex, housing and clothes. Jesus says we should focus less upon these things and focus firstly upon the kingdom of God and His righteousness. God promises to give us all of our basic needs and He implores us to place our complete trust in Him. "Which of you by taking thought can add one cubit unto his stature [Matt 6:27]."

The problem is that when we focus upon food, drink, sex and such the like, we cannot also simultaneously focus upon God. Whenever I am thinking about my next meal, I find it very difficult to concentrate and listen. The same thing happens when my mind wanders and meditates upon the things of this world. I find it very difficult to focus upon the things of God and the things of the world at the same time. You may ask what are the things of the world? The bible makes it clear that it is the lust of the flesh, the lust of the eyes and the pride of life [1 Jn 2:16]. An eye cannot look at heaven and at hell at the same time. Either he looks towards the heavens or he looks at the earth. Either he looks at God or he looks at the self. This is why Jesus exhorts us to place all of our trust in God for providing these needs; so that we might be able to better utilise our mind by remaining focused for the real task at hand.

We are different from the world because we are holy and set apart for God's glory and honourable use. We are set apart to focus on him and to focus upon him alone. This is what distinguishes us from the world which always focuses upon appeasing the flesh. "For after all these things do the Gentiles seek:) for your heavenly Father knoweth that ye have need of all these things [Matt 6:32]." We do not need to focus upon what God has already promised to provide us. We do not need to continue to focus upon earthly possessions which God has already told us he would provide in due course. Instead we must focus upon fulfilling his will and knowing him in a more intimate and deeper way.

Have you ever been in the immediate presence of somebody and yet found yourself feeling very distant to them? Say there are two of you in a room a husband and a wife and whilst the wife is talking about how her day at work went the husband is daydreaming about football, food and all of the other pursuits he has planned for later in the evening. He is in the room but he is not really present with her. His mind has wandered to another realm and he was lost all focus regarding her presence and her being, albeit temporarily. This is how we often are when it comes to the presence of God. It is so easy for us to read scripture, worship and praise, even speak about him in fellowship whilst we neglect the fact that he is always around and with us in the present.

This is something Jacob found out after he had a dream of a ladder ascending up to the heavens, with angels of God ascending and descending on it. "And, behold, the LORD stood above it, and said, I am the LORD God of Abraham thy father, and the God of Isaac [Gen 28:12-13]." God promised Jacob to give him the land he was standing on for an eternal inheritance for his seed. He also promised him that all of the families of the earth would be blessed in his seed. "And Jacob awaked out of his sleep, and he said, surely the LORD is in this place; and I knew it not [Gen 28:16]." From that day forward Jacob surely learnt that He is a God who is always around us at any given place during any given moment.

This realisation should make it easier for us to focus upon his presence at any given time, rather than being easily distracted like the husband who is in the room but not quite present with his wife. The reason why the husband was not focused on his wife is because he was too busy thinking about the future. This is what happens to any of us when we fail to be rooted and grounded in the present. When we look at what happened with Jacob before he had the dream of the ladder we see that he was too busy worrying about his life in the future. He had just escaped the threats of his brother Esau and he was very anxious about his future upkeep. But when he saw the LORD in a dream he received reassurance that God was near to him. His life was never the same afterwards and he subsequently began the journey of focusing on Him earnestly with faith.

After this experience with God Jacob promised to offer up a tenth of all of his substance unto God. I believe this referred to his material substance but I also believe we can offer up a tenth of our spiritual substance too. We can decide to offer up a tenth of our time everyday unto God: a time we can dedicate unto prayer, worship and the study of his word. This will require us to spend 2hours and 24 minutes each day, or 144minutes each day. This brought Jacob great reward and so will it with us. It will help us to focus on God, making him the most integral aspect of each of our decisions and motivations in life.

So often we fail to exercise focus because we are too busy focusing about the past or the future. God wants us to focus on the present presence of his Being. Not on what we will eat, what we will do, drink, wear or do tomorrow or later on, not on what we did yesterday, last year or even ten years ago, but the Lord wants us to focus on him and him alone in the present presence. This is the only way we can fellowship with him. In fact, this is the only way we can successfully fellowship with anybody: when we concentrate and pay attention to their being and what they have to say in the present tense.

The Eyes of The Lord

The scriptures says the eyes of the LORD run to and fro the whole earth to show himself strong on behalf of those whose heart are perfect towards him [2 Chron 16:9]. Solomon says the eyes of the LORD are in every place, beholding the evil and the good [Pro 15:3]. And in another proverb the king says Hell and destruction are before the LORD: how much more then the hearts of the children of men [Pro 15:11]. These scriptures encourage us that God is omnipresent.

When Hagar was being mistreated by her mistress Sarai, after conceiving with Abram, she fled from the family household and escaped into the wilderness. She was approached by an angel of the LORD who comforted her and told her to return home. Hagar was very startled by the revelation and she learnt that God was a God who not only saw all of the struggles, circumstances and worries we face in life, but also a God who cared about them. She must have once thought that he was an impersonal and uninterested God who did little to interact with the beings on his earth; but after she was comforted by his angel she received an even clearer revelation about his true nature. "So she called the name of the LORD who spoke to her, 'you are a God of seeing,' for she said 'truly here I have seen him who looks after me.' Therefore the well was called Beer lahai roi [Gen 16:13-14 ESV]."

God is very much focused upon what takes place on the earth. His eyes are not only looking at the external affairs of mankind but his eyes are also looking into the hearts and invisible parts of man.

When we look at God with our eye then our eye becomes one with his eye. This is the deepest meaning of 'let thine eye be single.' Jesus' eye was single with the eye of his Father. This is why he was able to say 'me and my Father are one [Jn 10:30].' It is because they were always focused upon each other. A wise man once said 'the eye which I see God is the same eye which God sees me [Meister Eckhart].' And another theologian has said something similar by observing how 'when the eyes of the soul looking out meet the eyes of God looking in, heaven has begun right here on earth [A.W Tozer, Pursuit of God].'

Cultivating Focus

Complete and devoted focus is not something which we can learn overnight but rather something which we can cultivate over time. Abraham is described in the book of Hebrews as a devout and focused man who "looked for a city which hath foundations whose builder and maker is God [Heb 11:10]." But Abraham was not born with this focus, but he cultivated it through his life experiences and encounters with God.

Abraham was seventy-five years old when he began his pilgrimage to Canaan. This scripture indicates that he should have arrived in Canaan much earlier in his life but when he travelled with his father from the land of Ur in Chaldea they stopped almost half way in Haran and settled there. It was not until his Father Terah had died that he continued on in his journey and finally settled in the land which God had told him to depart to. Abram was obedient in the end but perhaps he could have learnt more and accomplished more for LORD had he been more focused from the beginning.

When we lack focus we are likely to only go half-way and we will only put in a half-hearted effort. God wants us to put absolutely everything unto his cause so that we can glorify him with everything which is inside of us and leave this earth with no regrets and shortcomings. Sometimes he will require us to separate ourselves, as he did in the case of Abram, from our friends, families and common comforts found within our nation before he can cause us to focus solely upon him and thereby succeed.

But although Abram's journey was initially slow and somewhat abrupt he certainly developed momentum as he began to focus more and more upon God's vision for his life.

Here are some of the practical steps we can take in order to develop momentum as we learn to focus better.

(1) Pray ceaselessly - this keeps our mind focused on the presence of God

(2) Avoid procrastination at all costs

(3) Watch for Jesus' return

(4) Let everything you do, in word or deed, be done in the name of Jesus

(5) Approach Jesus with a pure heart

(6) Learn to listen better

(7) Avoid dwelling upon the past and future

(8) Remain rooted in the present presence of God

(9) Make friends with other like-minded focused people

Preparation

The consequences for a lack of preparation are severe.

"And that servant, which knew his lord's will, and prepared not himself, neither did according to his will, shall be beaten with many stripes." [Lk 12:47]

Preparation is key before we avail in anything we do in life. Before I sit an examination I must first prepare and revise. Before a boxer faces his opponent he must first prepare and train. Before I go to work each morning I must first prepare my attire. How much more then does this apply to the work of God?

Every single person who God has used in a mighty way has first had to undergo a season of preparation. They have had to prepare for leadership and they have had to acquire the suitable character needed to withstand pressure, possible persecution and other temptations which will certainly threaten to engulf them, before God has moved them centre stage. Without this preparation they would have likely crumbled at the slightest measure of opposition.

A man who seeks to construct a house does not do so overnight but he first plans the architecture over a substantive period of time and then progressively works upon the construction. The same applies to how God prepares us for his work. God is sovereign in preparing us for the work He has ordained for us. He is the Potter and we are the clay. He is the Master builder and we are the stones. All he requires is our obedience, patience and submission - and by the time we know it we will be found ready as "a vessel unto honour, sanctified, and meet for the master's use, and prepared unto every good work [2 Tim 2:21]."

There are a number of biblical figures who had to undergo extensive preparation before they were unveiled to the public for the work of God.

David had to endure at least a decade in the wilderness before he was exalted as the king of Judah and later Israel. The same observation can be made for the Lord Jesus Christ who we hear nothing of in the scripture between the ages of 12 until he began his ministry at the age of 30. These were known as the silent years: the time which he used wisely in order to prepare—in building up his character—before he began the work God had prepared for him. In the 2nd book of Chronicles we are given a short account of a king called Jotham who excelled much during his life upon the throne of Judah. The author makes it clear that his success was owed to his meticulous preparation. "So Jotham became mighty, because he prepared his ways before the LORD his God [2 Chron 27:6]."

When Kings go to war against their enemies they must prepare. It would be calamitous and unwise for them to send their troops to engage in costly and potentially deadly conflict without first equipping and training their troops. They would also have to send spies so that they might gain a clearer picture of the respective strengths and weaknesses of their enemies. Even football teams send out scouts to watch their next opponents before preparing for the next game. When Israel were approaching the land of Canaan God ordered Moses to send out spies to search the land before they went forward and took possession of the area which was promised to them.

Preparation is clearly key before we succeed in conquering any task. In the body of Christ there are a number of things we must prepare for before we begin taking responsibilities in the kingdom of God. We must prepare ourselves in character, in doctrine, in our lifestyle and in our relationship with God. We must also prepare ourselves against the schemes of the devil and we must learn how to react to different temptations and battles which will duly befall us.

When God raises us in his glory he also expects us to teach others how to be raised up too. Jesus would not have been able to teach his disciples about the kingdom of God unless he had first experienced it himself. We cannot teach anybody something we have not yet experienced ourselves. How can an unsuccessful boxer who has never prepared for a fight teach a young boxer how to prepare for a fight? We cannot teach other people about the things of God unless we first become well acquainted with the things of the kingdom of God ourselves.

One of the best examples of a man who had to undergo thorough preparation before being used by God was Joseph. Joseph had to prepare for his role in the Egyptian government for at least 13 years before God promoted him. But in the story of Joseph we find one key principle which underpins all successful preparation. Joseph knew he was going to be exalted by the LORD one day but he continually found himself in situations and difficult circumstances which appeared to oppose the vision which God had given him. First of all he was sold as a slave in Potiphar's household and secondly he was taken into prison for no fault of his own. But wherever Joseph found himself he continued to excel. In both Potiphar's household, and in the prison, we are told how "the LORD was with Joseph [Gen 39:2,21]." We are told that Joseph prospered in everything he set his hand to do and he was promoted both by Potiphar and the keeper of the prison. Joseph did not lament or sulk about the conditions he unfairly found himself in but instead he worked to prepare himself—both in character and intimacy with God—before he was promoted to the position God had promised him. This shows us that we have an opportunity in every single circumstance to prepare ourselves for the work which God has ordained for our lives. We should never let difficult circumstances prevent us from developing our character and preparing for the work at hand. But we should be confident that all things work together for our good no matter how inexplicable the circumstances which beset us may be at first. God is faithful and will surely complete the good work he has begun in you.

The main priority is walking with God and deepening our relationship with him. The best way to prepare for the work God has ordained for us is to seek his face with all of our heart and to discover the specific purpose he has for our life. This is vital because if you do not know what God has called you to do then how can you prepare?

Paul and Barnabas were ministering to the LORD, seeking him with great hunger and determination, ardently fasting and praying, when the Holy Ghost said "separate me Barnabas and Saul for the work whereunto I have called them [Acts 13:2]." If God can see that we are hungry to prepare for his work, then he will also entrust us with the authority and responsibility to execute his plans. But if you are not hungry or diligent in preparing for the work of God then how can God expect you to be hungry or diligent with the work itself? If Joseph was not diligent in the prison or in Potiphar's household could we have quite possibly expected him to be diligent in the household of Pharaoh? All of these men of God prepared for the work of God by first becoming intimate with God: who then helped them prepare —by giving them specific instructions—for the work which he had ordained. God does not leave us alone to prepare for the work he has set for us but he works with us to prepare. All he requires on our part is a steadfast desire to work with him in the meantime.

The same thing happened in the life of Elijah. In the first glimpse given of the prophet in the scriptures Elijah rebuked Ahab and declared that there would be no rain upon the idolatrous Israel for three years. Now we cannot imagine that Elijah arose to such prominence without any ongoing preparation. But he was certainly being prepared by God for his important ministry before he rebuked the King, although this is the first time we hear of him in scripture. When somebody arises to the scene suddenly we must remember that they must have prepared alone in the secret place before they were later revealed in the public place. Only those who prepare in the secret place are raised to prominence in the public place.

Whilst we wait for God to initiate the ministry he has prepared for us there are some things we can put into practise daily. We should not just be passive but we must be active before the Lord uses us mightily to undermine and destroy the kingdoms of darkness. Before the Lord Jesus ascended into heaven he commanded the disciples to stay in Jerusalem so that they might wait for the promise of the Holy Spirit [Acts 1:4-5]. They obeyed and did this but they did not remain passive in the meantime but they were actively proactive. "These all continued with one accord in prayer and supplication, with the women, and Mary the Mother of Jesus and with his brethen [Acts 1:14]." Prayer is a good practise to cultivate in the season of preparation. There are also other practises we can learn to develop in the meantime too.

(1) SOAK UP SCRIPTURE

When Jesus went to Jerusalem for the feast of tabernacles he went into the temple and taught the people. "And the Jews marvelled, saying, how knoweth this man letters, having never learned [Jn 7:15]." The multitude whom heard the Lord speak were all startled when they heard the words which went forth from his mouth. Jesus Christ was a very learned man and this shows us that he invested a lot of time in studying the scriptures before he began his public ministry. He never went to a bible school or studied under prominent Pharisees such as Gamaliel but he was well schooled in the word of God because he was persistent and consistent in his studies.

I can remember in my own journey how I would spend most evenings studying the word of God. I was tempted to go to bible school but I did not feel led to go there by God. So I continued to study the word of God although I did not necessarily have the best focus or understanding. Besides studying the word of God I had also began evangelising every Thursday. A couple of friends led me to a fellowship they were familiar with and when I arrived there the senior pastor began to prophesy into my life. I was startled by the grace of God that was present in the room and immediately God gave him a word of knowledge. God showed him that I was a teacher. He also prophesied a number of things into my life. One of the things that he foretold was that God would give me greater wisdom to understand the scriptures. He told me I would deepen my understanding of the scriptures in three months, but I received the gift before this time. I am sure God rewarded me for my diligence. He saw that I earnestly desired to know more about his word and because he is a rewarder of those who diligently seek him, he had no choice but to give me the gift sooner than I had anticipated.

If Jesus needed to learn the word of God and familiarise himself to the holy oracles of his Father in order to succeed and refute the various rebuttals of the enemies of God, then so must we. When Jesus began his ministry he was led by the Spirit of God into the wilderness to fast without food for 40 days. During this time he was tempted a number of times by Satan who attempted to rely upon scripture to cause the Lord's downfall. But Jesus rebutted the suggestions made by the devil by rebuking him with the correct application of scriptures. He used three scriptures to be precise, which were found in the book of Deuteronomy [Deu 8:3, Deu 6:16, Deu 6:13], and with these he was able to withstand the enemy's temptation.

It is one thing knowing the scripture but it is an altogether different matter to understand and apply it. I may know what a gun is, I may now about its design and about its construction, but if I have never used the gun and I do not have any experience of its use, then what would be the point of all my knowledge? My accuracy will certainly be well off the mark. Jesus learnt scripture during the preparation season but he also learnt how to understand them and apply them with godly wisdom. The same must surely be undergone by us so that we will be prepared to fight against the devil and all those religious characters who are under his influence.

(2) BECOMING MORE FAMILIAR WITH GOD

When Jesus Christ was baptised by John the Baptist in the river Jordan the heavens parted and the spirit of God descended down upon him in the form of a dove. "And lo a voice from heaven was heard saying This is my beloved Son, in whom I am well pleased [Matt 3:17]." Jesus had clearly been working on his relationship with God before he began his ministry. This is made evident to us in the opening remarks made in the gospel of Luke. At the mere age of 12 years old he went up with his family to Jerusalem to observe the feast of Passover. When it had finished he was accidentally left by his parents who had thought he was in the midst of the large group of people they had travelled with from Galilee. When they returned to Jerusalem they found him in the Temple learning and questioning the doctors of the Law.

"And all that heard him were astonished at his understanding and answers [Lk 2:47]."

Jesus had a good understanding of God because he had spent quality time with Him everyday. When his parents found him they were somewhat offended but he replied to them saying "how is that ye sought me? wist ye not that I must be about my Father's business [Lk 2:49]?"

It is important for us to know God in the preparation season, or to at least be working in the process of knowing him more. To know him in an experiential and intimate way is essential. We must learn to become familiar to his still silent voice and we must learn to adorn ourselves in his Holy Character. This is so important for only "the people that do know their God shall be strong, and do exploits [Dan 11:32]."

(3) DEVELOP CHARACTER

This is such an important criterion because we cannot glorify God with our gifts and spiritual talents alone. Jesus told his disciples "Herein is my father glorified, that ye bear much fruit: so shall ye be my disciples [Jn 15:7]." The fruit which our Lord alluded to was the holy character of God. We receive this by the grace of God's impartation as we spend more time under him and become gradually transformed by the daily application of his Word.

WE NEED NOT REMAIN COMFORTABLE ON EARTH

God does not want us to grow too comfortable upon this earth, especially when we are sojourners and pilgrims on a temporary mission. One of the main reasons why a believer or non-believer may be comfortable upon this earth is because they love too many of the attractions which it has to offer. The wealth, the luxuries, the indulgences and delicacies, there are many things which are found upon this earth which please the flesh. But God does not want us to remain satisfied by these temporary pleasures and neither does he desire us to depend upon that which is contrary to Him. For the scriptures says that if any man loves the world that the love of the Father is not in Him [1 Jn 2:15]. If we love the world then we will naturally want to abide upon it forever and rarely will we entertain thoughts and deep longings for the New Jerusalem which is beyond the horizon. However, if we despise the ways, customs and attractions of this world then there will be no particular reason why we want to abide upon it for too long. When we have finished our mission and glorified God why would we want to stay any longer upon an earth which is full of misery and pain when we can spend more time with our Father in a large place which is full of peace and bliss?

The Apostle Paul honestly told the disciples at the church of Philippi how he was facing a dilemma. On the one hand he desired to be with the Lord, which he considered to be the best option, but on the other hand he thought it necessary to remain upon the earth in order to help the younger disciples. Paul had a great desire to depart from his bonds on the earth and he earnestly thought it better to be with the Lord than to stay in this world. His desire to leave this world did not begin from his time in prison but preceded this: so we cannot attribute his desire to be with the Lord solely on the basis of the treatment he endured in the Roman jail, where he wrote the letter to the Philippians. But Paul desired to be martyred—so that he might be with the Lord—even before he was placed into bonds.

This is shown to us in the 21st chapter of the book of Acts. Paul and the disciples were tarrying in Tyre and had planned to go to Jerusalem. As they awaited the journey they fasted and tarried until one of the other disciples, speaking through the inspiration of the Holy Ghost, told them not to go there [Acts 21:4]. However, Paul still insisted on going. He knew he was going to face persecution there but he systematically deduced that this would not necessarily be a bad thing if he was to be martyred there as he so desired. The Apostle and the disciples tarried for a few more days in the house of Phillip the Evangelist when they were visited by a prophet called Agabus. When the prophet came to the home of the evangelist he went up to Paul, took up his girdle and bound his hands and feet, saying "thus saith the Holy Ghost, so shall the Jews at Jerusalem bind the man that owneth this girdle, and shall deliver him into the hands of the Gentiles [Acts 21:11]."

Now when the other disciples overheard these things they pleaded with him to stay and not go up to Jerusalem.

"But Paul insisted and told them that he was not only ready to be imprisoned but to also die for the sake of the Lord Jesus [Acts 21:13]." Paul was ready to go home.

Here are some of the contrasts which were likely to be considered by Paul when he was lost in his dilemma.

Remaining here:	Departing to be with Christ:
(1) Temporary residence, in a mere tent	1) A permanent abode
(2) Suffering mixed with joy	(2) Joy unmixed with suffering
(3) Suffering for a little while	(3) Joy for ever
(4) Being absent from the Lord	(4) Being at home with the Lord
(5) The fight	(5) The realm of complete deliverance from any form of sin
(6) The realm of sin	

The Apostle Paul is not the only man of God who had expressed such longings to leave earth and be in the immediate presence of the Lord. The author of the book of Hebrews says that Abraham was looking for a better country, a heavenly city which is above and not of the earth [Heb 11:16]. "He looked for a city which hath foundations, whose builder and maker is God [Heb 11:10]."

We are living in perilous times when God will surely begin judging the nations with his wrath. When we look at the conspiracy to abort children and to undermine God's sacred institution of marriage we will surely discern the times we are living in. We ought not to become so fond of this world when it will shortly be destroyed. "Seeing then that all these things shall be dissolved, what manner of persons ought ye to be in all holy conversation and godliness, looking for and hasting unto the coming of the day of God, wherein the heavens being on fire shall be dissolved, and the elements shall melt with fervent heat? Nevertheless we, according to his promise, look for new heavens and a new earth, wherein dwelleth righteousness [2 Pet 3:11-13]."

And how about the man of God Elijah who wanted to be taken from the earth prematurely? Elijah had just been victorious in a prophetic dual against the 450 false prophets of Baal who ate at Jezebel's table. But when word came to him that Jezebel was hunting him for his death he fled into the wilderness in desperation. "And he requested for himself that he might die, and said, it is enough; now, O LORD, take away my life; for I am not better than my fathers [1 Kin 19:4]." Elijah's request was answered by God eventually and he was taken by the LORD God in a chariot of fire through a whirlwind which took him into heaven [2 Kin 2:11].

The same story applies to our Lord Jesus. In the book of Hebrews we are told that "for the joy that was set before him [he] endured the cross, despising the shame, and is set down at the right hand of the throne of God [Heb 12:2]." Jesus understood that the great everlasting joy God had prepared for him would far exceed the shame and anguish he was suffering within a sinful world.

Now I am not saying that we ought to be completely miserable during our short lives on this earth. Rather the opposite! For there are a number of things to enjoy on this beautiful earth which God has created for us. Family, fellowship with the saints, God's vast and beautiful nature, and the reading of God's word, are just a few we could mention. But none of these fare in comparison to the majestic kingdom which God has prepared for those who love and obey him. When we walk in this understanding—namely that there is a better life for us on the other side— then we will dispel many insecurities. We will be more free of fear, free of dangerous fondness, full of boldness and dynamic productivity, and we will surely strive to work our hardest for the work of the Lord before our time on this earth expires. Whatever we sow upon this earth has eternal repercussions. We ought not to let our struggles overcome us and bring us into depression or suicide but rather we must strive to make the most of our time upon this earth doing the work of God before we return to the home he has prepared for us. We should be grateful for each new day.

I can remember the time I was first born again and I believed the Lord would return any day soon. I wanted the Lord to return and to establish his kingdom as soon as possible and I honestly believed that his impending second coming was to arrive soon. I was very watchful during this period of time and peculiarly zealous for the cause of Christ. I was far from being comfortable and my ardent desire to die daily, and to carry my cross, made a life with Christ in heaven a far much better option than remaining on the earth.

If we do not long for the return of Christ and we proclaim to be believers then there can only be two possible reasons for this. Either because we have yet to fulfil our God-ordained mission; or because we have become too comfortable in the world. If we are fulfilling the will of God and dying to ourselves and the flesh daily, then there should be no reason whatsoever why you would desire to stay on a earth unless you felt there was still much more to do for God. There would certainly be times where we cry out like Jeremiah "Cursed be the day wherein I was born: let not the day wherein my mother bare me be blessed [Jer 20:14]."

And if we are in Christ then we ought to "look for a new heaven and a new earth, wherein dwelleth righteousness [2 Pet 3:13]." We need not remain comfortable on an earth which is defiled with iniquity and obstinate to God's beautiful ways. Yes, we must strive to bring about God's kingdom in our communities and yes we must strive to compassionately win souls too, but we also ought to continue "looking for and hasting unto the coming of the day of God [2 Pet 3:12]." A day when we will be heavily recompensed and rewarded for doing the will of the Lord.

During this season, early on in my walk with Christ, because I honestly thought the Lord would imminently return I did my best to ensure that I was without spot and blemish, blameless and faithful to his cause. This drew me very close to the Lord and he showed me many revelations during this time despite my immaturity in the faith. This is because I was very hungry for him during this season and I longed to be with him in heaven, above all other things.

Love

God is love.

God's occupation is love.

God's presence exudes love.

Love is his nature and love is the way he draws souls to Jesus Christ. God wants relationships with lovers; people who will love him in Spirit and in truth.

God loves love. But if there is something which he loves even more than his love then it is lovers who love His love. This is why man was created: so that he could enjoy His love and reflect it back to Him who is the source of all love.

Love is a social thing. Love cannot be contained and it must be shared with others.

True love is reciprocal.

God is looking for souls who love Him regardless of what circumstances they face in life. Lovers like Abraham and Jesus who will be willing to sacrifice anything and everything to exemplify their sincere love for Him.

Love is not contingent upon circumstances in life. Love is transcendent and independent of all situations which take place within time.

Love does not look for a reward or a blessing in return.

Love is personal. And love is a communion between two individuals who become one by virtue of the communal love they share towards each other.

The most important commandment is to love God with all your soul, heart, might and mind. This means you must love God with the deepest depths of your inner man. Everything that you think, say, desire and pursue must be done with the love of God in mind. Every motivation and intention must be propelled by the love of God. Every work we do for Christ must be done because of the love of God. Good works are meaningless unless they are done from a place of genuine love. A wife may love to cook, love to clean, love to look after the children and do many other good domestic works, but what is the worth of all of these works in the grand scheme of things if she does not harbour any genuine love for her husband?

Many times we may fall into the religious trap of loving the works more than the person. This is idolatry. The main reason why we were created is to have a solid and loving relationship with God. If we were created in God's image and likeness and God is in Himself the substance of love, we too must be able to possess and share the love of God.

When we love somebody we want to become familiar with their presence. Love is something which is developed over time and not necessarily overnight. The more time we spend with somebody who we take a liking to the more likely we will grow in our love for them. The more time we spend in their presence—and taste of the goodness of their love—the fonder we will grow of them.

Love is the foundation of all solid relationships. If we do not love God we will find it very difficult to obey him. Especially when obedience requires us to take big sacrifices. Jesus always obeyed the Father because he loved Him. If we do not love God with the whole heart, we will find it difficult to always obey him. Judas loved Jesus but Judas loved money much more than his friend and so he betrayed him. Peter loved Jesus but Peter loved his own life more than his master so he also betrayed him. When we love something, anything, above God, then this is called idolatry. When this happens we face the inevitability of betraying God in exchange for the idol.

Idols are not necessarily physical images which are exalted upon physical altars but they can also be spiritual and mental images which are exalted in the altars of our hearts.

No man can serve two masters. Neither can there be two captains of the same ship. The same applies to our hearts. The master of our heart is either Jesus or something else. If it is not God then it is some other type of idol. This is not good in the eyes of the LORD for the first commandment is that "thou shalt have no other gods before me [Exo 20:3]." God understands how difficult this is because He says that the heart is desperately wicked and deceitful above all things. But God promised us that he would give us a new heart and that he would replace our heart of stone with a heart of flesh [Eze 11:19]. Therefore, we have an opportunity to change. God can help us change if we turn to him daily.

Love is a two-way relationship between at least two persons. So the love which God is inviting the body of Christ to share in is a requited and perfect love: not something which is one way and unrequited. The Father is calling us to love Him just as much as Jesus loved Him. Nothing more and nothing less. This may sound impossible at first. But in everything we should remember how nothing is impossible with God. It is the grace of God which enables us to love him with everything which is inside of us. If we want this grace we must simply ask him, but we must do so daily. God said we should ask and it will be given unto us according to His will. It is certainly God's will for us to love Him with all of our heart.

Imagine how peaceful and beautiful our world would be if everybody loved God. The kingdom of God is exclusive to lovers of God. But all of these lovers have received their ability to love God by His grace. For God is love. So God must fill Himself within the human soul for the person to actually love Him in the first place. Therefore, it is of grace, through faith, that we are able to love God.

We love him because he first loved us.

"Most men will proclaim everyone his own goodness: but a faithful man who can find?" [Pro 20:6]

"And the Lord thy God will circumcise thine heart, and the heart of thy seed, to love the Lord thy God with all thine heart, and with all thy soul, that thou mayest live." [Deu 30:6]

Man is born with an Adamic nature. This nature of the flesh makes him at enmity with the love of God. But when a man repents and chooses to follow Jesus he is now given the Holy Spirit which enables him to love the LORD. But every man has a decision whether to embrace the Holy Ghost or to reject it. When Stephen was rebuking the Sanhedrin he said "Ye stiffnecked and uncircumcised in heart and ears, ye do always resist the Holy Ghost: as your fathers did, so do ye [Acts 7:51]." Therefore we have a choice to embrace God's love or resist it. If we embrace it then God will gradually teach us—as he circumcises our heart—to love him with all of our soul.

Man has resisted the Holy Ghost from the days of Adam and Eve and he still chooses to do so today. When we receive the Holy Ghost God gives us the grace to love him more and more by an ongoing sanctification process which he works through us. But it is still possible for us to backslide if we are not careful. We must make the conscious and consistent effort to love God every day. If we do not do this then other cares in the world will take His place. We must therefore renew our minds every day.

If we make this our goal and our one sole desire in this life then we will surely excel. Whatever we focus upon manifests into reality in our lives. In other words, whatever we sow we will one day reap. If we continue to focus upon becoming lovers of God we will eventually become the great lovers of the Lord which God so earnestly desires. But if we focus upon other things in the world, even other religious works which are not necessarily bad in themselves, such as knowing the most scriptures, being the best preachers or becoming more prosperous, then whilst we will assuredly gain success in these pursuits which we focus upon, we will miss the most important pursuit of all in becoming a pure and sincere lover of God. This what Jesus was communicating to Martha and Mary. Martha loved God but she was too busy with many things and pursuits; whereas Mary had chosen the best part of life which was sitting at Jesus' feet, communing with him in pure adoration.

David was called a man after God's own heart. This means that he sought to have an affectionate relationship with God. David sought to discover what pleased God most and he was ever eager to seek the LORD for His perfect will. David wanted to please Him and he continued to do this to the utmost of his ability despite making a few mistakes on the way.

This is what lovers do. They strive to please one another. This is alluded to by the Apostle Paul in the epistle to the Corinthians when he outlines the expectations of covenant relations between husbands and wives. In his first letter to the Corinthians he makes the observation that a husband lives his life to please his wife and that a wife lives her life to please her husband [1 Cor 7:33]. This a great indication for the love they have for one another. Just like a mother who will do anything, even give up her life, for the sake of her children, so too will a faithful husband and wife who will do anything for each other to please one another. This is what God did for us through his Son Jesus Christ. He who knew no sin became a sin-offering for us so that we might have life and become the benefactors of God's love. He revealed his love for mankind by offering his life for our life. We must remember that the Lord Jesus is our husband and that we are his bride. Jesus gave his life to please his wife and we must therefore use our life to please him because he is our husband.

David understood this from a young age and so sought to do His will at every given opportunity. David understood the importance of prioritising God's heart, and His love, above all other things. He did not seek God as a means to an end but he desired the presence of God as an end in itself. He said in one of his psalms "the Lord is my Shepherd I shall not want" [Psa 23:1]. David did not have any other desire but close intimacy with the living God.

And in another psalm he said "One thing have I desired, this will I seek after, that I may dwell in the house of the LORD all the days of my life [Psa 27:4]." David only had one longing desire in his heart. To be accepted by God into closer intimacy. David is often called a man after God's own heart. David understood that God has a heart and he was determined to discover what pleased it. David also understood that God was a God who would favour those who sought for his heart. "I intreated thy favour with *my* whole heart: be merciful unto me according to thy word [Psa 119:58]." David understood the personal and relatable aspect of God. He wanted God to like him and he was successful in this pursuit.

"Howbeit the LORD God of Israel chose me before all the house of my father to be king over Israel for ever: for he hath chosen Judah *to be* the ruler; and of the house of Judah, the house of my father; and among the sons of my father he liked me to make *me* king over all Israel." [1 Chron 28:4]

He deserved this recognition as being a man after God's own heart for he had a deep and earnest desire to know and please God. However, the best example of a man who was also after God's own heart is the Lord Jesus Christ.

Jesus Christ always sought to please the Father and do his will. Not only sometimes or when he felt stirred to do so in the comfort of his home but during all circumstances, he wanted to please God. "Then said I, Lo, I come (in the volume of the book it is written of me,) to do thy will, O God [Heb 10:7]."

He never compromised in his life and he always strove to obey God. Jesus did not obey God out of religious duty or out of fear, but he obeyed God because he loved Him. He wanted to please God. He wanted God to smile and to be glorified. He did a perfect job by managing to achieve this. For God cried out, not only once, but twice that "this is my beloved Son in whom I am well pleased." God was pleased with Jesus not only for his obedience but more importantly for his pure and unadulterated love which propelled his obedience.

Jesus Christ was a man who was sold out to the love of God. He did not just preach about the love of God but he daily experienced the power of God's love. Jesus Christ's ministry was all about love for God and love for people. Jesus Christ was primarily a teacher of love. All of the works of healings, signs and wonders which were performed by Christ came from a place of abiding in God's love. They were not the priority or the goal of his ministry but they were an overflow of his love for God and people.

Works should never precede love for God. But works should always be worked from a place of love. Sometimes I hear people asking what Jesus was doing between the ages of 12-30. These are known as the silent years. I know what Jesus was doing. He was developing his intimacy with God. It was like the Father took him through the school of love and only sent him into the world, for his ministry, after he graduated with top honours. Jesus learnt what it means to love God before he was finally entrusted with the mighty works God had chosen him to walk in. The same thing happened with Joseph who was also exalted at the age of 30.

This gives us a clear lesson to learn. We must first learn to love God before we learn to walk in ministry. Too many ministers are entering work without sufficiently spending time with God and knowing Him.

God has planted a vision into their spirits but they are being born prematurely. A good teacher will teach you what he has learnt and experienced. But an illegitimate teacher will only pretend. A minister who has rushed into the ministry without sufficiently spending time with God is like a bride who is rushed into a marriage with a man who she has hardly spent time with or knows. Such marriages are often frail and fragile in comparison to marriages which have first undergone an engagement period.

Every great man or woman of God must first became intimate with God before they began working with him. Adam was created on the sixth day. The seventh day was the sabbath so Adam's first whole day was a rest day before he began working afterwards. This symbolises how Adam rested in God before he began to work. He thereby had to learn intimacy with God before he was sent to work in the garden. The same principle was at play in Moses' life. Moses did not suddenly step into the responsibility of becoming Israel's liberator overnight. But he grew in his knowledge and love of God for forty years in Midia first. David was a man who knew of God and loved him with a tender heart from a young age. But he still had to endure many trials and persecutions on his journey to the throne of Israel. David grew in his love, dependence and intimacy with God during this period. David had spent a lot of solitary time with God and he even began writing his psalms before he became the king. David was made king of Israel at the age of forty when God had felt he was now ready to represent God's love to His chosen nation.

Jesus Christ is calling us to be intimate with him before he sends us to do his work. Before he sent his disciples to preach the gospel, to cast out devils and to heal the sick, he called them to be with him and spend time with him [Mk 3:13-15].

If we spend more time with him we will grow in our personal love for him. Love is not just an idea or a concept but it is a substance of God's being. Love is not simply a feeling and emotion but it is a quality of character which indwells within an individual with permanence.

Love is not subject to change. It is independent of temporal circumstances which take place within the world.

God says he loves us with an everlasting love [Jer 31:3]. This means that the love which God loves us with is not dependent upon our current situation. We may have committed a sin but this does not mean God does not love us. We may be battling with pain or other un-ideal circumstances but God's love for us still does not change. When David committed grievous sins by committing adultery and murder God was clearly upset and very angry. But God still loved him with an everlasting love. And when Peter betrayed Jesus three times God still loved him. In fact, whilst we were yet all sinners Jesus Christ loved us. This is because God, in his high and lofty position of eternity, could already foresee the finished product we would one day become within the sphere of time. This is what God sees when he loves us with an everlasting love. Jacob was a man who made ample mistakes too. But God loved Jacob because he knew what Jacob would become even before he entered his mother's womb. God loved what Jacob would become in the fulfilment of time. Whereas God hated Esau because He knew how wicked and unrepentant he would become in the manifestation of time.

It is so important to love God first before we step into the perilous waters of ministry. I call it perilous because there will always be greater responsibility and condemnation to whoever takes the position of a leader. The apostle James acknowledged this when he admonished the church leaders to not become teachers over many things [Jas 3:1]. Leaders and teachers are directly in charge of directing the goals, purposes and destinies their students will take in life. If they teach their students anything else outside of the love of God, then most of their students will not learn about the love of God themselves. If their focus is towards religious practice, towards prosperity or any other pursuit outside of the love of God, then their students will become the products of what they sow. This is why it is so important that we learn how to love God first before we are then empowered to teach other people about the love of God. Because they become whatever we are.

The sons of Eli, Phineas and Hophni, were both working in the tabernacle as priests of the LORD. But the scripture recalls that they did not know the LORD, and that they were sons of Belial, despite having an important role to play in the ministry [1 Sam 2:12]. They were sleeping around with many women and misusing their religious power to eat forbidden flesh from the animal sacrifices. They were eventually killed by the LORD for their stubbornness and profanity.

A lover of God will obey the LORD even when difficult challenges arise and when temptations come flooding in. Abraham was willing to sacrifice Isaac because he loved God. Joseph was not willing to sleep with Potiphar's wife because he revered and loved the LORD. Jesus Christ did not complain when he was being greatly tested in the garden of Gethsamene because he loved the LORD. Paul was able to endure many persecutions—and to remain faithful until the end—because he really loved the LORD.

Sacrifice and love are deeply connected. They are involved in all types of relationships, because there is always a need for compromise between two parties whom are unlikely to ever have perfectly compatible views. God had to sacrifice his Son. And mankind has to sacrifice their own bodies and will. This is how the two began a relationship with one another: but the sacrifices on both parts are propelled by love. God sacrificed his Son because he loves us and we sacrifice our bodies unto God because we love Him.

Holy and Harlot

God is looking for lovers who approach him with a pure heart. These are men and women of God who desire nothing else but the presence of God's love. They do not desire God just because he is going to provide them with prosperity, with wealth, with power and any other earthly possession. But they come to God with an innocent and pure heart because they simply love his face. This is what the Holy Ghost means when he says Jesus is looking for a glorious church without spot, wrinkle or blemish [Eph 5:27].

It is so easy for us to envisage a wedding garment with spots, wrinkles and blemishes. But the wedding garment which is being spoken of here is an inner garment of the heart. To have blemishes, spots and wrinkles signifies a particular heart condition. It is used to symbolise believers who pursue God for the wrong reasons which are not found from seeking God for Him alone. To have a garment without spot, blemish and wrinkle simply means to have a pure heart. A heart which is focused and entirely devoted to having a loving and meaningful relationship with God. A relationship whereby she is submissive to God's word and is totally loyal and faithful to His great love. This is the Church which God is awaiting. So when the Apostle John documents how he sees the bride of Christ—who is preparing herself for her husband—come down from heaven, what he is really communicating to us is that he foresees a body of believers who have understood and fully perfected the purity of their hearts. This is clearly a process. Because there are many impure motives which can arise in our hearts when we begin walking with God and receiving his power.

When we begin walking with God and we are born again we are always like innocent children with pure hearts and intentions. But when we reach a more adolescent stage of our maturity other distractions and temptations certainly arise. Just ask David. King David was a man who had a pure and loyal heart when he first began walking with God in his youth. But when he received great power and blessings from the LORD he became lax and complacent. In his complacency he committed adultery with Bathsheba and subsequently murdered her husband.

David's heart was clearly impure at the time. Which is why in the psalm which he wrote in the immediate aftermath he said "create in me a clean heart, O God [Psa 51:10]." David clearly recognised the need for maintaining a pure heart. A pure heart can quickly become impure in much the same way an impure heart can quickly become pure.

We must therefore guard our hearts at all times and make sure we are diligent to keep them purified every day.

We may ask 'how do we know that they are purified?' The easiest way for us to discern the state of purity is when we can unquestionably acknowledge that all we desire upon this earth is a loving relationship with God through Christ Jesus. When we desire nothing else in this world and we are not pursuing anything else but the will of God for our lives then we can be certain that our heart is currently pure. Doing a 'good work' is not good in itself if it is done from an impure motive. A good work is only good when it is done from the pureness of your heart in love. A good work is only good when it is done in alignment with God's will for your life.

Jesus Christ had to deal with many religious hypocrites who sought out God for the wrong reasons. Jesus knew their hearts and understood that they were only using the name of God to pursue their own ulterior motives. Jesus said that they loved special honour and attention from men [Matt 23:7]. They loved to be seen of men and they enjoyed the authority they received from the adhering congregations. They loved the honour they received from their congregations and the great respect the community held in their esteem. They worshipped the LORD with their lips and honoured Him with their mouths, but their hearts were far away from Him.

Jesus was generally dismayed by their approach to religion because he could see through their false pretences and he understood that they were using the name of God as a means to secure vainglory. We have to guard our hearts to ensure that we do not make the same mistakes. Every time we do seek God we need to reflect within our hearts and ask why am I seeking Him. We need to think about what we think and desire.

"There are many devices in a man's heart [Pro 19:21]" and the heart of a man is naturally deceitful and wicked. It is so easy to seek God for the wrong reasons. We may see how God has blessed other believers— how they have been blessed with prosperity, a large following, a successful ministry and so on and so forth—and in our covetousness seek out a relationship with God to receive these blessings too. This is not true love for God. But this is a love for the blessings and possessions which God gives us as a result.

Do not get me wrong. There is nothing wrong in loving God because he has blessed you abundantly. Of course we should! But this should not be the main motive for seeking him. We should only seek him for the sake of seeking his face alone. And the only blessing we should desire when we seek his face is his love and companionship. If we seek him for anything else outside of this then we are no different to a goldigger.

A goldigger is a woman who forms relationships with a man purely to obtain money or gifts from him. If we seek God to obtain money and any other form of material blessing from him then we are no different to a goldigger. This will make God displeased and he will eventually punish you for your idolatry of heart. Think of the narratives of Balaam, Simon and Judas. For if we seek God in order to receive something other than God then this simply means that we love something else above God. This is idolatry and the Bible makes it clear that no idolater will have his portion in the kingdom of Heaven [1 Cor 6:9].

The severity to which God feels about this spirit of the goldigger cannot be underestimated. God shows us how serious he feels about it when the Lord Jesus went into the temple and overthrew the tables of those who sold oxen, sheep and doves. Jesus was so wroth when he saw the people buying and selling in his Father's house. He made a scourge of small cords and drove out all of those who sold the merchandise outside of the Temple. "And said unto them that sold doves, Take these things hence; make not my Father's house an house of merchandise [Jn 2:16]."

Merchandise is sold to make profit. This indicated that the people in the Temple at Jesus' time were only visiting the proximity of God's house in order to benefit their pocket. They did not have genuine and pure motive in entering the vicinity of God and nor did they desire to submit to him in whole-hearted worship. They used the house of God as a means to secure material benefit for themselves. This is what made Jesus so frustrated. Their main priority was not intimacy with God but material gain and worldly profit. God was simply a banner, a means to an end to secure their idols. God was not treated as a person or as a Lord but as a mere name or idea, an ideal and stepping stone to help them secure their own ulterior motives.

We must ask ourselves whether we do the same today. Why do we go to church and why do we pray to God? What do we pray to God for and what is the reason why we request for certain things from God? Do we seek God because of the material blessings He may provide us with or do we seek Him because we sincerely love Him and want to please Him?

I can remember a time when I only went to church because I had become obsessed with a girl I had come to like. I wanted to marry her and I thought she would have been my ideal wife. I did not initially attend the church: but I was working in a bar which did functions and would regularly host church fellowship. One shift I happened to be working in the room where they hosted one of these fellowships. The service was about the Holy Spirit and I spotted her immediately. She was weeping as the Holy Spirit touched her heart and for some strange, irrational reason I began to believe that she was my ordained wife.

I love when I see people weep for the Lord, it shows a sincerity of heart and I know how I have felt when I have felt led to do so myself, so when I saw her weeping I thought she must have had a good heart. She was also very beautiful so I was convinced that she would be a suitable match. I wanted to take her number down but I opted against it in the last moment. Luckily there was another lady who was in the leadership team who I knew; so she took my number and she asked me to join them a few weeks later. I was glad she did and I had planned to come to another meeting when the next opportunity arose. Perhaps a door would open in the future for me to pursue my desire I thought. So when the opportunity arose a few weeks later I jumped optimistically through the open door and when I saw that she was there I was relieved and hopeful.

To tell you the truth I did not get many opportunities to pursue the relationship that I desired. I went to church week after week with the hope that I would muster up enough courage to eventually ask her out. But I didn't, well at least for a very long time. In time I began to actually enjoy the fellowship. The Church was welcoming and I felt like a member of the family. The discussions were called life groups and they were very enriching. I became a regular and a recognised face. I actually enjoyed the praise and worship too but I could not help but recognise that I also harboured a secret motivation. I wanted to get to know this girl! And I made no intention of hiding it from God either because I continued to pray, almost daily, for him to reveal his will to me regarding the matter.

Eventually I grew very frustrated and impatient. I was unsuccessful and when I did finally make a move, she was uninterested and unresponsive. I had come to realise that my heart felt like it had become split in the middle. I had lost some of the initial fervour of love, sincerity and purity of love which I had once shown to God. I had quickly become double-minded and I was arguably only attending church because I wanted to find my wife.

There is a significant message in the epistle of James which deals with this problem and it is called double-mindedness. It is like we have two minds or two hearts which are incompatible: a mind for the world and a mind for God. We have one foot in the world and one foot in the heavenly. One foot with Satan and one foot with God. One foot in unrighteousness and the other foot in holiness. Half a heart of selfishness and half a heart of service. Such a position is untenable to maintain.

This is clarified a number of times in the word of God. James makes a number of points which are linked to this problem. He admonishes the church to purify their hearts lest they become double-minded [Jas 4:8]. He also informs us that friendship with the world makes us an enemy of God; that if we become too fond of the world we are no different to adulterers and adulteresses [Jas 4:4]. James is trying to exhort the church to remain pure and single-minded. It is impossible to please God if we are otherwise.

If I put my money into two business ventures, then I will not be as focused as if I place all my time into one business. Or if I am a manager of two different football teams, say a domestic league team and a national team, I will certainly find it more difficult to be successful with both teams at the same time. Similarly, we cannot be successful when we split our attention, time and energy along two opposing sides. The kingdom of God and the kingdom of the world are diametrically opposed. So it is nonsensical for us to approach God in order that we might receive something which He is opposed to. God is against the lust of the flesh, the lust of the eyes and the pride of life. We cannot therefore go to Him in order to receive these things.

"Ye ask, and receive not, because you ask amiss, that ye may consume it upon your lusts [Jas 4:3]." Not only will God be unhappy when we seek him with an impure heart but he will also ignore these requests which we so often selfishly pester him for. God is looking for children who are pure in heart and who want him solely for his abiding and liberating presence. Just like Moses when he said I will not leave unless you give me your presence [Exo 33:15]. Moses could have requested for so many things, and I am sure God would have provided anything for him, but Moses was only interested in receiving a deeper level of intimacy and revelation of God. With such, God is well pleased.

God is looking for lovers who demonstrate their love for Him by only asking for His perfect will to be done in their lives. He is looking for lovers who please Him in all that they do. He is looking for lovers who want to glorify His name and receive greater intimacy with Him here upon this earth. Anything else makes us no dissimilar to the men who bought and sold merchandise in the Temple.

Daily I must reflect upon my heart and question my motives. I make it my objective to seek God and him alone. I look at the Apostle Paul and think of him as an exemplar role model. He said he considered everything in this world as dung apart from the knowledge of Jesus Christ. He said he was not concerned with the things which had taken place in his life beforehand but he was only concerned with pressing on forward to attain a deeper depth of intimacy with Christ. This desire stemmed from his love for God. This had to be the case because we only want to spend significant amounts of time with people we love.

I had a friend who was like those who sold and bought merchandise in the temple. I love him and I am sure he loves me too but sometimes I cannot help but suspect that he loves me for the wrong reasons. He is always asking for money from me. I do not particularly mind giving him money but he does not really offer me anything of value in return and there have been times where I have suspected that he was only using me. He does not particularly respect me, he has spoken evil of me a few times, sometimes he acts funny and distant from me and I cannot help but believe he is somebody who takes advantage of the generosity which God has placed within me. Sometimes I have to ask myself 'is there anything which I gain in return from walking with him; and if not is there any point in continuing the friendship?'

We have to ask ourselves the same thing when it comes to our relationship with God. What does God gain in return from our relationship with him or are we only walking with him because of the material benefit we can receive from him? We should never underestimate the value we can provide to God. All good relationships are built upon mutual value and benefits. We benefit from an endless amount of things from God. But it is easy to forget that God also benefits from having a relationship with us too. We are God's glory and His means by which His name is honoured and glorified upon the Earth. Moses walked very closely with God. When his face shone like the sun God was glorified too and not Moses alone. When he used the prophet to part the Red Sea God was glorified again. The same applies to Jesus when he performed many miracles.

"Even everyone that is called by my name: for I have created him for my glory, I have formed him; yea, I have made him [Isa 43:7]."

There are a few friends whom I have, who have clearly exhibited the glory of God in their lives. It is so easy to focus upon their talents and gifts when they perform a powerful work of healing or when they preach. But when I reflect upon their works I always recognise in the end that it is God who is working through them to execute His power. This is how God glorifies His name. This is one of the principal ways God benefits from his friendship with man.

But when I was walking with my old friend I could not really recall one benefit I received from our friendship. Now I am not saying that we should seek relationships with one another because we are *only* aiming to secure certain benefits. This would not be a real friendship. But what I am observing and saying is that all good and stable friendships are marked by mutual value. The mutual value shared between a man or woman of God and the Father is always spiritual. We benefit from God in our relationship with Him because he provides us with love, peace and purpose; and God benefits from His relationship with us because He is glorified and His word is vindicated through what He achieves in us. But in my 'friendship' with the guy I have alluded to before, only he received benefits from our relationship and they were mainly material. This is why the relationship could not last for too long and this is also why many relationships between believers and God do not last for too long too.

How many of us today are only seeking God because of the material benefits he can provide us with? I wanted to terminate my friendship with this person. The same principle will apply with God for those who do likewise. The children of Israel were only interested in God when they wanted Him to provide them with food, meat and water. When God came down on mount Sinai they were all afraid and did not want to initiate a closer relationship with Him. "So the people stood afar off, but Moses drew near the thick darkness where God was [Exo 20:21]."

They did not respect Him nor revere Him. There was nothing in return which they would offer God, not even their obedience and submission. In his displeasure God therefore terminated his relationship with many of them in the wilderness. He said to Moses "I will make you a nation mightier and greater than they [Deu 9:14]." God sought to replace them and did exactly that. This is how I felt with my old friend. I wanted to find a friend who would mutually value and benefit my life.

All We Need is Jesus

I can remember one day when God clearly tested my heart. I was talking to one of my friends on the phone about the Lord. We were just talking about personal relationships and how to hear the voice of the Lord. After we had been speaking for some time I proposed for us to pray before ending the call. I prayed for him first and I prophesied quite a few things into his life. I also prayed for a lot of spiritual benefits which I wanted him to receive. And then it was his time to pray for me. Now I was expecting him to pray for some time, at least thirty seconds or so, hopefully for more I thought. I also expected him to pray for a number of things for me to receive. However, I was quite taken aback by his response. His prayer was about three seconds long and he thanked God for only one thing. He literally said to me "I thank God that Modupe has Jesus" and that was it!

I cannot lie — at first I felt a bit silly. I had been praying and prophesying for so many things for my friend but he ultimately showed me that only one thing was needed. JESUS!

I had been praying for so many things for him. I had been praying for success, for wisdom and for greater knowledge. I prayed that he might receive a prophetic unction. I prayed for his relationships with other people. And I somewhat expected him to replicate the same thing for me. But all he did was thank the LORD that He had given me Jesus. Everything which I had been praying for his life was found in Jesus and I could have spared a lot of time if I had simply prayed for him to be filled with encounters with Jesus. I quickly started to understand that it was and is still all about Jesus!

After we stopped speaking on the phone I thanked God for what he had ministered to me through my friend. I understood that the only thing I needed was Jesus. And now I began to question my pursuit with God. Had I been seeking a relationship with God for the wrong reasons? To receive a popular ministry, more wisdom and knowledge, and even a greater share of the gifts of the Spirit so that I might look more powerful? I certainly had. And now I was forced to question the motives of why I had been seeking the gifts of the Spirit and the populous ministry. Was it because I wanted to be seen by men or was it because I had a genuine concern for the salvation of souls? I believe that it was a combination of both of these reasons. So when my friend prayed that short prayer for me it reminded me of the one thing I needed in life. An authentic and intense relationship with the Lord Jesus.

The episode is reminiscent to the story of Martha and Mary. I was like Martha God had been showing me. This is something I am reminded almost every day. Martha was distracted with much serving [Lk 10:40] whereas Mary was focused on knowing Jesus. It is important for us to remember that knowing Jesus is more important for us than doing works for him [Matt 7:21]. We must also beware of focusing too much on our ministries at the expense of focusing upon God. This is what Martha did. Mary on the other hand was praised by Jesus for choosing the one good part that would never be taken away from her. This was her deep love for the Lord Jesus and the intimacy which arose as a result.

Lovers

There are a number of indicators which help to reveal whether we are true lovers of God or not. When I felt God minister to me on this subject I felt Him lead me back to a close relationship I shared with a girl a few years back when I was in the world. I was able to learn so many important principles in such a short period of time when He drew me back to this past experience. Here are some of the things which God showed me that lovers love to do.

(1) LOVERS LOVE TO SPEND TIME WITH ONE ANOTHER: ALONE

This is what we know as the secret place. It is in contrast to the corporate functions when we pray and worship God together in a community. It is when we are solely alone with God, just you and Him, and it is usually manifested in prayer, praise, worship and the study of the word of God. God values secret time with us more than He does corporate time: just like a husband and wife—who are deeply intimate with one another—will surely prefer to spend time alone in secret more than they do with all of their friends and family in public.

There is much more that they learn about each other when they are alone than when they are in a public environment. There are some things they can do in private which they will be prohibited to do in a public place. And they generally prefer the things that they can do in private, in their intimacy, than the things they can do in public in front of other people. A married couple can make children when they are intimate together in the secret place. They cannot do this in a public place. They do not become one in the public place but they become one in the secret place. This is when a man knows his wife. This is when he becomes intimate with her within the bedchambers.

God wants to know us in the secret place too. This is the only way we will be able to bear His fruit. For a man and woman cannot have the type of intimacy which bears children when they are in a public place, when they are in the company of other people; but they can only do so when they are spending intimate time together in the secret.

One of the most popular stories in the bible is about a certain wrestling match which took place between Jacob and a mysterious man. Jacob had previously fled his ancestral home after stealing the birth right and blessing from his older brother Esau. He had been sent to his uncle Laban by his mother and father because Esau was exceedingly wroth and sought to kill him. After twenty years of labour, many more children and much more life experience under his belt God had finally told him to return to the geographic location of his old home. But Jacob had to first settle his conflict with his brother and he was understandably scared. Jacob cried out to the Lord and sought for His helping hand as they passed over the ford Jabbok.

"And he rose up that night, and took his two wives, and his two women servants, and his eleven sons. and passed over the ford Jabbok [Gen 32:23]." Jacob sent his wives, his children and his concubines over the brook and remained in solitude with the Lord. "And Jacob was left alone; and there wrestled a man with him until the breaking of the day [Gen 32:24]."

What followed next is one of the most important events which have taken place in human history. Jacob was left alone in prayer when he was met by a mysterious man who approached him. Jacob wrestled with the man all night and in his tenacity and steely determination he refused to let go. During the wrestling duel Jacob had his thigh broken but he refused to let go. The man he was wrestling with pleaded with him to let him go but Jacob told the man that he was not willing to let go unless he would be blessed. The man asked him what Jacob's name was and when the patriarch replied the man changed his name to Israel and blessed him there.

"Jacob was left alone" when he was blessed by the man. Jacob called the name of the place Peniel which means the face of God. This means that the man whom Jacob wrestled with was a similitude of the Lord himself. But let us not detract from the most important observation here: namely that Jacob was left alone when he first wrestled with God and was subsequently blessed by Him. Jacob's name was changed to Israel and he was told by the man "for as a prince hast thou power with God and with men and hast prevailed [Gen 32:28]." Jacob was later blessed by the Lord himself and when he did meet his older brother Esau he found favour and peace from the man who had previously sought to kill him.

This brief episode communicates many profound lessons. It teaches us the deep value and riches which are received from spending alone time with God. We will first receive power with God and then with men. This is because God is power and when we become one with him we receive the fullness of his power over all things which are subjected to him.

When Jacob had wrestled with the man all night he was later commended for prevailing. We will also prevail in all things when we take the time to wrestle with God. The power which God gives us as we wrestle with him in prayer empowers us to prevail over sin and the death which transgression warrants. Jesus destroyed the works of the devil and death because he was empowered by the Spirit of God to do good at all times and to overcome all forms of sin. Jesus received this power because he spent most of his life alone with the Father. Before Jesus began his powerful ministry he spent 40 days alone in the wilderness with the Father. When he was released by God to begin his ministry of deliverance he was empowered by the Spirit to undermine and unshackle the works of the devil. But Jesus still needed to retire regularly into the wilderness to be alone with God in order to be replenished from the virtue which left his body during his great healing crusades.

When Jacob wrestled with God he was later blessed. God will also bless us when we spend regular alone time with Him. God blesses and favours those who seek his face. The place where Jacob wrestled with the man is called Peniel which means the face of God. Because Jacob sought the face of God all night he was blessed. There are a number of spiritual blessings we too can receive from God when we spend time with Him in the secret place and seek His face. One of the most profound blessings is the spirit of revelation. This revelation can be manifested in a number of different ways. The revelation can be in reference to the word of God or it may be a specific word from God which is given to us about our own lives and circumstances. I can testify that many of the revelations I have received from the word of God have come through private study with the Lord in the secret place. The same applies with private words which I have received from God to affirm his hand of blessing in my life, and the personal plans he was in store for my destiny.

Jacob said to God he would not let him go until God blessed him. Jacob wrestled with Him until the dawn of day and he was subsequently blessed in the morning. This indicates that Jacob was persistent, determined and perseverant. He didn't get his blessing straightaway, but because of his patience and his determination, he reaped the blessing in the morning. Wrestling has connotations of struggle and personal contact. Sometimes we may struggle to spend sufficient time with God in the secret place. We may struggle to retain personal contact with God on a daily basis. But if we persist, as did our patriarch Jacob, then God will surely bless us in many different ways.

This is what happened in the life of Abram. Whenever the LORD appeared to Abram and promised to bless him, he always appeared to be alone with Him [see Gen 15, 17].

When we spend time alone with God he will share with us specific instructions and words of edification which are needed for our personal growth. When Moses first began his ministry and heard the LORD God speak to him from the burning bush, he was alone [Exo 3:1-4]. And when Moses spent 40 days on the mount alone, after leading the children of Israel out of Egypt, God gave him specific instructions on how to build the tabernacle [Exo 24:18-40]. When Elijah was alone in a cave by mount Horeb God gave him specific instructions too. The prophet was instructed by God to anoint Hazael of Syria, Jehu to become the new king of Israel and Elisha to replace him in his stead [1 Kin 19:15-16].

God is willing to give us very clear instructions when we tarry for Him in the secret place. God gave Jesus specific instructions when the Lord tarried in prayer all night before choosing his disciples [Lk 6:12-16]. When Jesus saw Nathaniel for the first time he testified to the young disciple how he saw him under the fig tree [Jn 1:48]. Nathaniel was astounded and understood how the Lord had seen him in the realm of the Spirit before he encountered him in the flesh. Jesus is likely to have experienced this during prayer with God.

Spending time with God in the secret place is so important for direction. God can certainly use prophets and other members from the body of Christ to clarify God's vision for your life. But their word should only be a confirmation of what God was shown you already in the secret place.

(2) LOVERS ARE ALWAYS FOCUSED ON ONE ANOTHER

Lovers are always thinking about one another. Not a minute will pass by without a thought for her love. She is focused upon him and in everything that she does or say she will always have him in remembrance. She is absolutely besotted with him and she cannot take him out of her mind. She wants to please him, and him alone, so she honours him by ensuring that he does not leave the arena of her mind.

A husband is upset whenever he spots his wife looking at another man or spending more time with her other friends than she does with him. This is exactly the same way Jesus feels when we are not focused upon him. Jesus said that a person can commit adultery in their heart when they lust with their eyes upon a particular person. The same applies to the bride of Christ when she lusts upon anything else which is not found in our Lord Jesus. No man will be pleased if his wife is always looking at other men and not at him. The same principle applies to us: when we look upon anything else which is found within this world apart from God. The lust of the eyes is one of the lusts we are exhorted to reject upon our sojourn on this earth. The lust of the eyes is dangerous because it diverts our attention away from the need to preach the gospel and remain holy. The eyes can only look at one place at a time. Either they are focused upon Jesus or they are focused upon the world. If our eye is single—that is they are focused upon Christ—then our whole body will be filled with light. But if they are not single our body will be filled with darkness and how great the darkness will be [Matt 6:22-23]. The lust of the eyes is not restricted to sexual desires but it can also embody a vast array of different pursuits. This can include a lust for wealth, power, honour, popularity and vainglory. But Jesus is seeking a faithful bride who will keep her eyes looked upon his glory. In fact this is the only way that she might be transformed into his image. The Apostle Paul said "we all, with open face beholding, as in a mirror the glory of the Lord, are changed into the same image from glory to glory, even as by the Spirit of the Lord [2 Cor 3:18]." It is insufficient for us to glare at Christ momentarily if we want to undergo change. But we must abide, we must stare at him at every moment, if we want to see the transformation which God desires. Jesus said a city which is divided against itself cannot stand [Matt 12:25]. If we are divided by what we focus upon then it will be impossible for us to endure until the end. What you focus upon is the thing which you will eventually build. If we focus more upon the things of this world than we do of Christ then we will build a construction which is in the world and not in heaven. The homes which are on earth will one day be uprooted and burnt in the fire. But the mansions which are erected in heaven will stand forever.

(3) LOVERS COMMUNICATE

Lovers are open with one another in communication. They are always speaking to each other, all throughout the day, and they openly and confidently reveal the contents which remain within the depths of their heart to each other. Lovers do not hide anything from one another but they regularly confide with each other, offering practical solutions to overcome some of the situations they may find themselves engulfed in.

There are some secrets, experiences and issues which can only be shared between lovers. There are some things a wife cannot tell her natural family or her friends but which she chooses to confide in with her husband alone. These are some reflections which take place within many intimate relationships and I can testify of this because I had one. She was my girlfriend. We were together for three years and I am certain that we spoke to each other everyday. We would text throughout the day maintaining a constant bond of conversation and if we were given the opportunity we would speak to each other on the phone or meet up in person. Most of my day was spent in communication with her and when we broke up it was a big shock to my system because I no longer had somebody to speak to as much! There were some family issues she was going through, some serious and sensitive issues which she felt obliged to confide in with me; and the same applied to me. She would cry before me and voice out all of her anxieties and worries before me and I would do the same. We were honest with each other and whenever we found any problems within our relationship we spoke to each other frankly to resolve the conflict amicably.

God requires the same with us. He wants us to open up to Him in prayer and to confide in Him with everything. When we do this God also confides with us: he gives us practical solutions to combat our concerns and he will also reveal his heart and mind about certain circumstances and questions where we require His guidance. Whenever I was in my intimate relationship with my girlfriend I would usually confide in her before confiding in anybody else. God wants us to always confide in Him first before we seek counsel from anybody else. The best way we can do this is by seeking and studying His Word. We should also speak to him in prayer, speaking to him as we would do to any other person.

The bride of Christ has access to the presence of God through the holy of holies by the precious blood of Jesus Christ. When he gave up the ghost on the cross the veil of the temple was torn in two from top to bottom [Matt 27:51]. This was not coincidental but it occurred because God was communicating to the Church that we are now able to enter into His presence by the holy blood which was shed as an atonement for our sins. We can now enter boldly before his throne in time of need to confide in him and receive grace and mercy. God is always open to our cries and concerns and he is more than able to offer practical solutions by his holy Spirit when we seek him. We are encouraged to cast our cares upon Him because He cares for us and He is always looking to speak to those who have open ears.

The first epistle of John lets us know how the anointing we have received from Christ abides in us and teaches us all things [1 Jn 2:27]. We do not need to confide in another when we can first confide in Him who is the perfect teacher and counsellor of all things. If we are unable to discern the will of God immediately when we ask Him a question we must always resort to his Word. When we read the Bible it is like God is speaking to us through the pages. It is easy for many of us to read the Bible like we are reading some historical document or a philosophical/ethical treatise, but we must always remember that the Bible is the active word of God. Whenever we read the Bible we are therefore listening to the words of God and we are thereby communicating with Him. But in our communication with Him we should always remember that it is better to listen than to talk [Jas 1:19]. So we must do less requesting and petitioning and do more meditation and reading. God will certainly speak to us if we are willing to listen to him.

But we must be honest with ourselves and ask ourselves whether we speak to Him more than we do with others. If Jesus is our spiritual husband then we ought to speak to him more than we do with anybody else. This is possible and it is not difficult by any means. We must learn to cultivate the skill of praying ceaselessly. The more we commune with God the more we will feel his presence. And when we have tasted of His presence we will surely crave more and more. This is why it is so important to pray ceaselessly and to keep in constant communication with God. If we are not communicating with God then we are usually communicating with somebody else. And if we are communicating with nobody then we will certainly leave a door open for the enemy to entertain our idol mind. The only way we can entertain the presence of God is by communication. And if we do not entertain the presence of God then we are entertaining the presence of some other type of spirit.

There are different ways we can continue to communicate with God. We must practise these daily and consistently throughout the day in order to remain before the face of God. Praying, worship, praise and reading the scripture, evangelising and fellowship, continuous meditation and focus upon the throne of God, all of these activities are communication in one form or the other, and they should be exercised diligently no matter how arduous they may be at first. When we do this we will experience the continuous outpour of God's love.

Lovers are Loyal

When me and my old girlfriend first got into a relationship we expected absolute faithfulness and loyalty. I suppose this was only natural because most meaningful relationships must be built upon the foundation of exclusiveness. God expects the same with his Church. He does not desire a bride who commits spiritual adultery with the world and He wants her to remain untainted and unblemished from the pollutions which are found in it. The pollutions of the world are categorised under the lust of the flesh, the lust of the eyes and the pride of life [1 Jn 2:15-16]. God wants us to desire him and long for him, to love him and cherish him, far above any of these lusts which are found in the world. God wants us to lust after him alone. When a man or woman commits adultery they are polluting their own temples (bodies). The same principle applies to us when we commit spiritual adultery against God. We will pollute the temple of the Lord. Now this is no light matter because the Word makes it clear that God will destroy those who destroy his temple [1 Cor 3:17]. Neither shall adulterers have their place in the Kingdom of God [1 Cor 6:9]. Spiritual adultery is therefore a grave sin we must avoid. All sins which take place do not much damage to the body but he that commits fornication or adultery directly damages his own body [1 Cor 6:18]. Spiritual adultery does not only profane the name of the Holy One of Israel but it also has a seriously detrimental effect upon our own bodies.

God is just as jealous as any husband over his wife. In fact I will go a step further to say that he is even more jealous. God is willing to forgive us when we repent but if we choose not to do so then we will not enter into the kingdom of God. I can remember when me and my old girlfriend broke up for a few weeks and then we later discovered how we had both slept with another partner during this short time we had split up from one another. We were distraught with one another and at first we did not want to reconcile. But we loved each other and we promised each other that we would remain faithful to one another from then on. God is upset when we are unfaithful to Him. But because he loves us he is willing to forgive us if we repent and promise to be faithful for the rest of our days. In a world when there is duality—where there is a life of light and a life of darkness, a life of righteousness and a life of unrighteousness—we must choose which side we want to remain faithful to. If we are not faithful to God then we are faithful to something else and if we are not for God then we are against him. If we are not faithful to God then we are faithful to his enemy. God is exceedingly jealous and wroth when we decide to place our allegiance to the devil; especially when he has already sent his only begotten Son to redeem us from the hold of that old serpent. Imagine if a man's wife commits adultery with his worst enemy. Imagine if he is a king and his wife has committed adultery with one of his adversaries—who is a younger prince attempting to stage a revolution. What do you think the king would do? I am certain he would burn both of them with fire.

Loyalty and faithfulness is the true mark of love. If you truly love somebody you will remain faithful to them even when continuous and strong temptations arise. Joseph was a man who was loyal to God. When Potiphar's wife tempted him daily he refused and rebuked her saying "how then can I do this great wickedness, and sin against God [Gen 39:9]?" Joseph chose not to sleep with Potiphar's wife because he was loyal to God and realised that in doing so he would compromise his faithfulness towards God. It was an attractive offer which was being flaunted before him daily but he reject it because of his faithfulness to God. We will likewise face daily challenges, temptations of the flesh and attractive offers of the world; but we have the power to reject them as Joseph did. Only when we reject them can we be found faithful in the sight of God. We will all be tempted at some stage, this is only certain. James says "blessed is the man that endureth temptation: for when he is tried, he shall receive the crown of life, which the Lord hath promised to them that love him [Jas 1:12]." James said "when he is tried." So he will be tried but how he responds depends upon how much he loves the LORD.

One of the practical steps we can take to remain faithful with God is to fellowship with other like-minded believers who are also loyal to God. When we spend time with them they will stir, motivate and inspire us to become more faithful with God. When we look at the light and blessings which God has bestowed upon them because of their loyalty we will be incentivised to follow suit in our lives. But if we spend a lot of time with individuals who are more predisposed to spiritual adultery then we will learn from them and walk as they do. This is what happened in the life of king Solomon. He was a mighty man of wisdom who was initially faithful to God. But when he married many strange women he came under the hands of their influence and began to serve their gods. The scriptures inform us that "when Solomon was old . . . his wives turned away his heart after other gods: and his heart was not perfect with the LORD his God, as was the heart of David his father [1 Kin 11:4]."

Lovers Submit

Offering God

One of the most assured ways to discern whether we love God is when we continue to live and comply in accordance to his perfect will. Lovers love to give one another gifts and presents. Think of the story of Mary of Bethany who gave the Lord Jesus a pound of ointment of spikenard, very costly, and anointed his feet and head [Jn 12:3]. The oil cost the woman a whole year's wages but she still chose to give him the generous gift. This is how we know that she must have loved the Lord. I know that somebody loves me when they give me something; for true love compels me to sacrifice something towards you. I know that my mother loves me because of the sacrifices she has offered me in life. She has sacrificed her time, her resources, her home, and many other things to express her love for me. The same applied to my old girlfriend. The same applied to Abraham when he sought to sacrifice his son Isaac to God. And the same applies to Jesus who sacrificed his own life for us so that we might have life and life more abundant.

Love compels us to give. Love is not an eerie emotion or a temporary, idyllic feeling. Love is functional and the fruit of love is giving. God showed his love for the world by sending his only begotten Son into the earth so that whosoever would believe in him would have eternal life [Jn 3:16]. God showed his love for mankind that whilst we were yet sinners Christ gave his life for us so that we might be forgiven. God shows us his love by sending forth the Spirit of his Son into our hearts. For God so loved the world that he gave us every spiritual blessing in heavenly places in Christ. For God so loved the world that he gave us eternal life.

God's love is expressed in his continual propensity to give. God's love is not in word but it is in deed. God loves us with his words and with his deeds. God's deeds are the fruit and proof of his love towards us. God gives us more things than we could possibly count. This is how we know that God loves us. But how can we know and show that we love God? The same principle applies in our lives. If we love God we must show it to him by what we give him and not by what we say to him alone.

If we love God the first thing we will give him is our obedience. Afterwards we will give him our worship and praise. And after this we can start to give him our utter devotion, attention and submission. The next thing we must learn to give God is our reverence. We must also give him our adoration and our whole heart. We must give him our time and focus. We must essentially give Him our whole being. "And now Israel, what doth the LORD thy God require of thee, but to fear the LORD thy God, to walk in all his ways, and to love him, and to serve the LORD thy God with all thy heart and with all thy heart and with all thy soul [Deu 10:12]."

We must give our all to God to show him that we love him. God has given us his all [that is his life]. "Hereby perceive we the love God, because he laid down his life for us [1 Jn 3:16]." God perceives the love that we have for him when we decide to lay down our lives for him.

Our bodies must be given as a sacrifice to God; we must show him that we are continually available to be used by him. Our wills must be given to God. Our tongues, our feet and all of our resources must be offered to God. Everything must be given to Him for His glory. This is what God did to show us that he loves us so we must do the same to mirror the deep love that he has for us. It is written that greater love has no man than this that he lay down his life for his friend [Jn 15:13]. When a father dies he gives all of his possessions to his son and the son becomes the heir of all his property. This is what happened when the Father led the Lord Christ Jesus to die on the cross so that we might become co-heirs and inheritors of his vast kingdom. If we consider ourselves to be a friend of God we must lay down our own life and give it all up to God.

The most noble thing we can continuously give to God is our will. If we love God then we will continue to say 'not my will be done but let your will be done in everything that I do'. This is what we really mean when we say we give everything to God. For everything that we are, and everything that we own, is embodied in our will. Jesus showed us the way we should walk when he offered all of his will upon the altar. Jesus Christ gave God his time, his intimacy, his resources and all of his will. Jesus Christ was and is the best exemplar of a man who truly loves God. He showed this to all men by what he gave to his Father. Jesus Christ has shown us that we will obey God if we love Him. But he has also enabled us to see that whosoever says they love God and does not do what he commands is a liar who does not abide in the truth.

Love is Superior to Works

There is a great difference between works from a place of duty and works from a place of love. Jesus Christ does say it is our duty to do good [Lk 17:10]. But to do works from a place of love will always be superior to doing good from a place of duty. God calls us to do good from a place of love. If I do good from a place of duty rather than a place of love then this implies that I am only doing good because I feel compelled to do good and not because I necessarily want to do good. Religion is filled with people who only do good because they feel compelled to do good. A husband and a father may only go to work and stay at his home because he feels obliged to do so from a sense of duty but such a position will always be inferior to a father and husband who wants to work and stay at home because he loves his children and his wife. The sense of duty the first man harbours toward his family could always subside or completely disappear, which may eventually compel him to leave his family when times become difficult. But a man who loves his family will stay loyal to them no matter what opposition or difficulties he may face in life. Duty is subject to change whereas love is immune to any opposition. Love is resistant to all forms of confrontation and love is steadfast amidst any opposition. Love is resistant to all trials and adversity and love persists during the most hostile of environments. Love is transcendent and it is not ruled or influenced by any reward or wage. Love is immutable and does not wane or increase depending upon environmental changes.

Doing good from a sense of duty is called religion whereas doing good from a place of intimacy is called love. The main reason why Jesus' ministry was so distinguished from the Pharisees and scribes whom opposed him is because he moved from a place of intimacy rather than a place of duty. When Jesus spoke the word of God he spoke with great authority and zeal. This was compared to the scribes and Pharisees who knew just as much scriptures than Christ. And yet all were astounded when they heard the boldness and authority by which Jesus spoke. Jesus spoke in this way because he was passionate about his Father's cause. He loved righteousness [Heb 1:9] and wholeheartedly sought to see his Father's kingdom established upon the earth. This was in sharp contrast to the Pharisees who spoke the word of God for a number of different reasons but did not even have a close relationship with Him. For some it was for honour of men and for others it was for vainglory and power. They used the name of God as means to secure their own selfish lusts, using the mantle of duty as a means to retain their own powerbase. This shows us how acting from a place of duty will always be subordinate to acting from a place of love. When I act from a place of duty it is often because there are certain wages and rewards which are accompanied with the duty. A soldier in the army will always be more effective when he is fighting from a sense of patriotism in comparison to a soldier who is being compelled by the government to fight for the nation.

Some act in accordance to religious duties because of fear and because they want to escape persecution and malign consequences from sin. Some do good religious duties because they will receive glory from men and worldly promotion as a result. Their intentions may have been pure at the start but when they saw the opportunity to cash in they became allured by ulterior motives. Think of Judas: I'm sure he was initially attracted to the purity of the Jesus' cause in the beginning; but when he saw that the ministry was making a lot of money then his intentions became corrupted. Another good example of this would be Gehazi, the servant and assistant of the man of God, Elisha. A man called Naaman who was the captain of the Syrian host was sent to Elisha in order to be cured from his leprosy. Elisha told him to dip himself in the Jordan seven times and when the captain obliged he was miraculously healed. Naaman was shocked, relieved and understandably wanted to reward the prophet. But the man of God declined the offer. This did not please his servant Gehazi who coveted the reward. "Gehazi the servant of Elisha the man of God, said, Behold, my master hath spared Naaman this Syrian, in not receiving at his hands that which he brought: but, as the LORD liveth, I will run after him, and take somewhat of him. So Gehazi followed after Naaman [2 Kin 5:20-21]." Gehazi lied to Naaman and told him that Elisha had sent him to collect a talent of silver and two garments. Gehazi coveted the gifts and took them home. But when he stood before his master Elisha he was already found out. He was rebuked by the prophet and received the punishment of leprosy from the LORD as a result. He was a clear example of somebody who hides under the banner of religion for selfish reasons.

A person who works for the LORD from a place of love and intimacy will not necessarily desire any earthly accolades or rewards. He or she will be like Elisha and will typically turn down worldly status and recompense to focus upon bettering their relationship with God.

Some comply with religious duties because they simply want to fit in and avoid confrontation. This is what Esau did when he took Mahalath the daughter of Ishmael to wife. Esau had already taken two wives beforehand, Judith the daughter of Beeri the Hittite and Bashemath the daughter of Elon the Hittite, but when we later saw that these two were a grief of mind unto his parents Isaac and Rebekah, he sought to make amends [Gen 26:34-35].

"And Esau seeing that the daughters of Canaan pleased not Isaac his father; then went Esau unto Ishmael, and took unto the wives which he had Mahalath the daughter of Ishmael Abraham's son, the sister of Nebajoth to be his wife [Gen 28:8-9]."

Esau only married this woman because he wanted to fit in and be accepted by his family. He desperately yearned for their approval after his younger brother Jacob had supplanted both his birthright and blessing, and having understood that Jacob would take a wife amongst his own kindred, Esau carefully sought to rectify his past mistakes by engineering a marriage alliance which would be more palatable to his family.

None of these reasons can be compared to doing the good for the sole reason of being rewarded with the love of God alone.

In the book of Revelation Jesus Christ addresses seven churches. One of these churches is the church of Ephesus and in his admonition to them he emphasises the greater value of love over religious works of duty. He begins his message by commending them for their works, for their labour and their patience [Rev 2:2]. He also commends them for their discernment and their disapproval of false doctrine. He says they have great patience and zeal to do his work; he is also impressed by their steadfastness and their continual triumph over lethargy. Such is their commitment and their determination to labour for the cause of the gospel that they have refused to faint during adverse and confrontational circumstances. On face value they look like the perfect church, without spot and blemish, which the Apostle Paul had worked so diligently to prepare for the Lord. However Jesus found fault in one thing, something which he would later claim was the most important work of all.

"Nevertheless I have somewhat against thee, because thou hast left thy first love. Remember therefore from whence thou art fallen, and repent, and do the first works [Rev 2:4-5]."

We can do all of the outer, external works in the world which Jesus Christ commands his disciples to do [such as evangelism and reading scripture], but if the inner work of complete and unfeigned love is neglected all of it means nothing in the sight of Christ. Jesus says that many will come to him in the day of his return justifying themselves before him with all of their religious works. He warned us that he would tell many of them to depart from him because he never knew them [Matt 7:21-23]. These are surely they who love the work of Christ over the person of Christ. They love religion in place of intimacy. They have neglected fellowship with the holy Spirit and have always worked from a place of religious duty.

When you love somebody you will want to spend time with them to get to know them better. But Jesus is rebuking those who have come to love the works more than him who has told them to do the works. This is idolatry, unless we do the works solely because we love Christ as a person.

This is what the Apostle Paul communicates to the Church at Corinth in the famous 13th chapter of his first epistle to the Corinthians. This chapter is often read in context of showing charity/love to other people. This is not an inaccurate interpretation but the Holy Ghost is also leading Paul to discuss the love that a Christian must also show towards God in order to bear good fruit. So when Paul is saying if I have the gift of prophecy, the knowledge of all mysteries and the gift of tongues; when he is saying if I have all the faith in the world so as to remove mountains, "but have not love, I am nothing," what he is really saying is that if I do not love God, and yet I excel in all of the gifts of the Spirit, this would not matter at all. For I would still be nothing in the sight of God if I did not earnestly love him. And if I were to give all my goods to feed the poor and give my body to be burned, but had not love, it would profit me nothing. So even if I performed one of the most heroic of religious deeds and yet did not do it from a place of love it would still not profit me anything. For only love covers a multitude of sins. There have been Buddhist monks who have burnt their bodies for religious and political protests. But this did not profit them because they did not have the revelation of Jesus Christ and nor did they love the one true God. The only way any of our works will profit us is when we love God with all of our heart, might, mind and souls. This is what God has always desired and in a world and in a time where hatred and angst is growing ever higher towards the heavens, does not God desire a Church who can shine the radiance of his love amidst a world consumed with enmity?

The reason why works do not suffice in pleasing God is because we can do a number of good works for a number of reasons which do not necessarily involve God. I could be doing good works to look good in front of other people; I could be doing good works to give me inner peace and to convince myself of my own righteousness; I could be doing good works to receive favour and good report from other people; I could be doing good works because there is an opportunity to make good money from it; I need not do good works because I love God. Many people do good religious works without any knowledge of the LORD and will they enter into heaven? Lest they repent and believe in the blood they will surely perish. When we read this, it may sound pretty harsh. But according to the way God has ordained we can only receive eternal life when we have an experiential knowledge of the Father and Jesus Christ [Jn 17:3]. So we see that good works taken alone cannot suffice in pleasing God. But God is looking for those who do good works from a place of genuine and faithful love.

Servants act from a place of duty whereas Sons act from a place of love and intimacy. But a servant is not an heir of the inheritance. Jesus Christ calls us to be his servants first but then he encourages us to walk as his friends and sons [Jn 15:14-15].

In the story of Isaac and Ishmael, Abraham sent the son of the bondwoman out of his house and only Isaac became the heir to his father. Abraham had other children with his wife Keturah but these sons were not the co-heirs with Isaac.

"Abraham gave all that he had unto Isaac. But unto the sons of the concubines, which Abraham had, Abraham gave gifts, and sent them away from Isaac his son, while he yet lived, eastward, unto the east country [Gen 25:5-6]."

This is allegorical for what God will do to those who obey him from a place of duty in comparison to those who obey him from a place of love. Those who obey God from a place of love are his sons whereas those who do so from a place of duty are his servants. The promise is reserved for those who love God in spirit and in truth. Jesus says that they will inherit all things [Rev 21:7], even as Abraham gave all that he had unto Isaac. But even as Abraham decided to give his other sons only gifts, so too will the children of duty only receive gifts. The gifts which the sons of the concubines received were temporary wealth, riches, cattle, honour and the like. And these are the same temporary gifts we will receive if we follow God religiously from a place of duty and without genuine love. Judas followed the Lord and received many gifts and accolades for his religious devotion. The same applied to the Pharisees and Sadducees. But they were stripped of all these gifts upon their death and many did not inherit the promise of everlasting life, which is the inheritance God promises to His Sons.

God will also test us to see what is really in our heart. He will test us to see whether we really love God for who is in Himself or whether we love Him for the things which he provides for us in His goodness.

"And thou shalt remember all the way which the LORD thy God led thee these forty years in the wilderness, to humble thee, and to prove thee to know what was in thine heart, whether thou wouldest keep his commandments, or not [Deu 8:2]." It is easy for any of us to love Christ in word and in tongue action but God wants us to love him in deed and in truth. Sometimes God will intentionally let us go through adverse circumstances so that he can test our heart and see whether our love for him is genuine or not.

Self Love as a Conduit to Love Others

God also commands his church to love his neighbour as he loves himself. This means he must love himself first for if he does not love himself he will not be able to love his neighbour in any meaningful sense of the word. Or to put it in another way if he does not love himself but actually despises himself then he will end up despising his neighbour too.

We cannot go onto love our neighbour unless we have the love of God dwelling inside of us. God is love and He is the only one who can love somebody properly.

So if we do not have God indwelling inside of us then we cannot love ourselves nor our neighbours. When we receive the Holy Ghost inside of us then we can love one another by virtue of God's grace.

So the first step towards loving our neighbour is loving God. This is important because we will only walk with the Holy Ghost when we love God. Jesus said we must obey him if we truly love him. And when we obey him we will be loved by the Father and indwelt by him. "If a man love me, he will keep my words: and my Father will love him, and we will come unto him, and make our abode with him [Jn 14:23]."

The scriptures say that it is God who works within us both to will and to do of his good pleasure [Phi 2:13]. Jesus said the same thing when he said that the works which he did he did not by his own might or strength but by the Father who dwelt within him [Jn 14:10]. Similar sentiments were reflected by Peter and John when they healed the lame man outside of the Temple of Jerusalem shortly after they received the Holy Ghost on the day of Pentecost [Acts 3:12-13].

This is the concept of grace. The concept of grace is not exclusive to the new Testament. Moses recalls how Noah found grace in the sight of God [Gen 6:8].

God told Moses "I will be gracious to whom I will be gracious, and will shew mercy on whom I will shew mercy [Exo 33:19]." In the book of Romans we read of how Abraham received grace from God because of his faith towards Him [Rom 4:16]. And there are a couple of other stories which help to elucidate the principle of God's grace: that without God's grace we cannot become righteous nor love our neighbour as we do ourselves.

This was made evident to a king who did not particularly know the LORD but experienced Him one night in a dream. Abraham and Sarah sojourned in Gerar after Sodom and Gomorrah had been destroyed. They stayed with the Philistines and their King Abimelech took a liking to Sarah. Because of Abraham's fear he lied to the King—as he had previously done to Pharaoh—and told him that Sarah was his sister. Abimelech believed Abraham and took Sarah into his harem. But God appeared to the king in a dream by night "and said to him, Behold, thou art but a dead man for the woman which thou hast taken; for she is a man's wife [Gen 20:3]." Abimelech was startled. He protested to the LORD and asked Him whether it would have been fair for Him to kill a righteous man and nation for one man's mistake. After all it was not his fault Abraham had lied to him, Abimelech protested. "In the integrity of my heart and innocence of my hands have I done this," the king protested [Gen 20:5].

The LORD rebuked him sharply, and reaffirmed to him that it was Him who had made him withhold himself from Sarah.

"And God said unto him in a dream, yea, I know that thou didst this in the integrity of thy heart; for I also withheld thee from sinning against me: therefore suffered I thee not to touch her [Gen 20:6]."

It is God's grace which prevents us from living a sinful life even today.

In the books of Jeremiah and Ezekiel God spoke of a time when his people would receive his grace through a new covenant. The inheritors of this new covenant would receive the law in their inward parts and have it written within their hearts [Jer 31:33]. And in the book of Ezekiel God foretells how "I will give them one heart, and I will put a new spirit within you; and I will take the stony heart out of their flesh, and will give them a heart of flesh [Eze 11:19]." A similar act of grace was spoken of by Moses in the book of Deuteronomy when the prophet wrote to the children of Israel saying: "the LORD thy God will circumcise thine heart, and the heart of thy seed, to love the LORD thy God with all thine heart, and with all thy soul, that thou mayest live [Deu 30:6]." All of these promises are given to us by our faith in the Lord Jesus.

Now that we have become recipients of his grace we must necessarily abide in God to continue loving our neighbours. We abide in God by walking by faith in the Lord Jesus.

We can only love one another if God, who is love, gives us the power and grace to do so. Thereby God is glorified in all good and righteous deeds He manages to perform through us.

Idolatry

God Cannot Walk with Idolators

God cannot walk with us if we have idolatry in our hearts.

One way we can discern idolatry in our own hearts is when we love anything else above and more than God, His Spirit and His Word. If we love anything above the pursuit of wisdom then we have idolatry in our hearts.

Another way for us to discern whether we have idolatry in our hearts is if we are thinking about anything else other than God more than we think about him on his throne. Idolatry can be extended to family members and close friends, or even our ministries and religious works. If we love and think of any of these pursuits, or people, more than we think of the actual person of God—manifested in the flesh of his son Jesus Christ—then we will fall culpable of succumbing into idolatry. Jesus Christ made this evident when he said "he that loves father or mother more than me is not worthy of me: and he that loves son or daughter more than me is not worthy of me [Matt 10:37]."

If we love other things more than we love God then we will not experience the fullness of His power and love.

The severity of idolatry is clearly communicated to us in the story of Exodus after the children of Israel were punished for fashioning a golden calf. God had mercy on his people and he sent his angel to guide them into the promised land. But he refused to be in their midst because of their idolatry. "I will not go up in the midst of thee; for thou art a stiff-necked people [Exo 33:3]" said the LORD.

God's presence cannot be in the midst of a person who is idolatrous.

Idolatry of the heart must be purged before we can regularly walk with God.

We can continue to ask God to change our natures into the nature which was exhibited by Jesus Christ. God is looking for men and women after His own heart who long and crave for the continual presence of God, whether they be in the church or outside of the church. He is not far from those who love him above all things. Not only is He within them but He is also upon them.

The Golden Calf

"And when the people saw that Moses delayed to come down out of the mount, the people gathered themselves together unto Aaron, and said unto him, Up, make us gods, which shall go before us; for as for this Moses, the man that brought us up out of the land of Egypt, we wot not what is become of him [Exo 32:1]."

Whenever we read a passage or story in the Old Testament we should always attempt to draw a parallel with our walk with the Lord Jesus. This is important because whereas the old Covenant cannot save man today, the new covenant—which is secured by faith in the blood of Jesus Christ—certainly can.

Every passage in the old Testament is a shadow of things which were, and still are, yet to be. The promised land is a shadow of heaven. The tabernacle is a shadow of the Temple of God which is in heaven. The sacrifices of bulls, goats and lambs were a shadow of the blood of Jesus, the sacrifice which takes away the sins of the world. And the Levitical system of priests were a shadow of the eternal order of Priests which is the priesthood of Melchisedec.

When Moses abode on the mount for a long period of time the children of Israel grew impatient and wanted to move on by themselves. They gathered themselves and went up to Aaron, "and said unto him, Up, make us gods [Exo 32:1]." They did not want to wait for Moses whilst he received instruction from God. Moses was on the mount receiving a number of instructions from God [most notably about the tabernacle which was to be built] and the people sought to enter into the promised land without his guidance.

The impatient children of Israel managed to persuade Aaron into acquiescing into their demands. "Aaron said unto them, Break off the golden earrings, which are in the ears of your wives, of your sons, and of your daughters, and bring them unto me [Exo 32:2]." Aaron was as much of a perpetrator than them. He did not show any semblance of resistance. And we can only imagine that he enjoyed the heightened sense of attention and power he was receiving at the absence of his brother Moses. The children of Israel brought Aaron their earrings and he "fashioned it with a graving tool, after he had made it a molten calf: and they said, these be thy gods, O Israel which brought thee up out of the land of Egypt [Exo 32:4]." If Aaron did not already cause enough damage, he also decided to build an altar before the golden calf and proclaim a feast day to the gods.

"And they rose up early on the morrow, and offered burnt offerings, and brought peace offerings; and the people sat down to eat and to drink, and rose up to play [Exo 32:6]."

Moses and Aaron were given the responsibility of leading the Israelites out of the land of Egypt and into the promised land. The LORD brought down a number of spectacular signs and plagues upon Egypt before freeing the children of Israel from the firm hand of Pharaoh. The LORD even divided the Red Sea and engulfed the chariots of the enemy within it. God sent quails and manna from the heavens and he sent Moses to strike a rock to quench the thirst of his people. But when the LORD descended in fire upon mount Sinai the children of Israel "said unto Moses, speak thou with us, and we will hear: but let not God speak with us, lest we die [Exo 20:19]." They were not motivated or interested by the possibility of intimacy: "the people stood afar off, [whereas] Moses drew near unto the thick darkness where God was [Exo 20:21]."

Moses had spent significant time upon the mount. It was not the first time he had been commanded by God to ascend it. But in the latest ascent, where he received instruction for the construction of the tabernacle, he spent 40 days and 40 nights. It was upon his latest stay that the children of Israel fashioned the idols. "And the LORD said unto Moses, Go, get thee down; for thy people which thou broughtest out of the land of Egypt, have corrupted themselves: they have turned aside quickly out of the way which I commanded them: they have made them a molten calf, and have worshipped it, and have sacrificed thereunto, and said, These be thy gods, O Israel, which have brought thee up out of the land of Egypt [Exo 32:7-8]."

We must ask ourselves and be honest, how many of us—like the children of Israel—have fashioned out our own idols, as we await the descent of our Lord Jesus? The children of Israel had grown impatient with Moses as they awaited his descent. In their impatience they fashioned themselves idols.

Are there any of us—who like our spiritual forefathers—have grown impatient with the descent of Christ and subsequently fashioned our own idols? The Old Testament is a shadow of things that are to precede the second coming of Christ. And Moses is a foreshadow of the man who brought about the new covenant, " the mediator of a better covenant, which was established upon better promises [Heb 8:6]." Moses was up on mount Sinai for a period of time before he made his descent and our Lord Jesus Christ is on another mount, mount Sion, for a period of time before he makes his descent [Heb 12:18-24].

When Moses was up on the mount Aaron acquiesced to the children of Israel's requests and fashioned them a golden calf. This event is a shadow of what is taking place today. For there are a number of Aaron's, a multitude of so called religious leaders whom not only acquiesce to our desires to serve other gods and idols, but who also help fashion them. "For the time will come when they will not endure sound doctrine, but after their own lusts shall they heap to themselves teachers, having itching ears [2 Tim 4:3]."

These are very rarely gods of stone, wood or gold but they are gods and idols which are placed within our hearts. Money, wealth, popularity, power, women, any sort of idol or object of desire which we place before God. God's first commandment is "thou shalt have no other gods before me [Exo 20:3]." A god is anything we worship, serve and praise before God. Do we ascribe worthiness to anything above God and His Word? We can be a 'god' in our own eyes and we can worship, serve and praise ourselves even over God. This is what many people do today, they are lovers of self more than lovers of God. Just like the children of Israel who "sat down to eat and drink, and rose up to play [1 Cor 10:7]," they are lovers of the flesh and despisers of those things which are holy and right.

The golden calf is a symbol for false religious practise. It is a symbol of spiritual fornication and perdition. The golden calf is also mentioned in the days of Jeroboam, the man who was chosen to succeed King Solomon as the King of Israel. During this time the nation had just been torn into two kingdoms—the southern and northern kingdom—and Jeroboam was the king of the Northern territories, whilst Solomon's son Rehoboam, was the king of the southern tribe Judah.

During Jeroboam's reign he constructed two religious centres in the land of Israel, in Dan and in Bethel. The king did this because he was fearful that many of his people would "go up to do sacrifice in the house of the LORD at Jerusalem whereupon the king took counsel, and made two calves of gold and said unto them [the people of Israel] it is too much for you to go up to Jerusalem: behold thy gods, O Israel, which brought thee up out of the land of Egypt [1 Kin 12:28]."

God had ordained his house in Jerusalem to be built. The temple was to be continually attended to by the Levites for worship and observation of certain rites and feast days which were to be held there. However Jeroboam created a counterfeit system. He "made priests of the lowest of the people, which were not of the sons of Levi. And Jeroboam ordained a feast in the eighth month, on the fifteenth day of the month, like unto the feast that is in Judah . . . so did he in Bethel, sacrificing unto the calves that he had made: and he placed in Bethel the priests of the high places which he had made [1 Kin 12:31-32]."

There is a certain and particular way in which God desires to be worshipped and there is another, counterfeit way in which most of mankind seeks to worship God. Cain sought to worship the LORD in the way in which he thought was best but only Abel worshipped the LORD in the way which God had ordained. Saul worshipped the LORD after God had already rejected and replaced him [1 Sam 15:31]. Paul thought he was serving and worshipping the LORD when he was a zealous Pharisee who persecuted the church. And there are countless other examples even today which show us the insufficiency of man's worship towards God. Are any of us like Saul worshipping the LORD in ignorance, oblivious to the fact that God has already rejected our sacrifice like he did unto Cain?

Jesus had something to say regarding this problem. This is what Jesus said to the Samaritan woman by the well:

"Ye worship ye know not what: we know what we worship for salvation is of the Jews. But the hour cometh, and now is, when the true worshippers shall worship the Father in Spirit and in truth for the Father seeketh such to worship him [Jn 4:22-23]."

The main reason why the children of Israel fashioned the golden calf is because they lacked patience. The children of Israel suffered from unbelief. Patience and faith are deeply connected. If you have faith then you will have patience, but if you do not believe and trust in God then you will also lack patience.

Abraham is a great example of a man who God was able to use mightily because of his sincere faith. God had promised the patriarch to be the father of many nations but both he and his wife were very old when they received this promise. They were also childless when this prophetic declaration was made. However, "being not weak in faith, he considered not his own body now dead, when he was about an hundred years old, neither yet the deadness of Sarah's womb. He staggered not at the promise of God through unbelief, but was strong in faith, giving glory to God [Rom 4:19-20]."

Abraham waited for twenty five years until God fulfilled the promise he made to the patriarch when he was seventy five. This was a clear testament of his faith and patience.

"For when God made promise to Abraham . . . after he had patiently endured, he obtained the promise [Heb 6:13-15]."

Faith produces patience.

But when we lack faith then we will naturally lack patience.

If we lack patience then we will revert back to our old patterns and way of life. This is what happened in the life of the Israelites as they departed from Egypt. Saint Stephen said of them: "in their hearts [they] turned back again into Egypt [Acts 7:39]." God had promised the children of Israel many things: that they would be a kingdom of priests and a holy nation, that they would be highly exalted above all of their enemies and nations of the world. but because they lacked the patience God had expected them to show, they decided to revert back to their own sinful ways.

"And they made a calf in those days, and offered sacrifice unto the idol, and rejoiced in the works of their own hands [Acts 7:41]."

Patience is a key virtue. God will not provide us with the things we want straightaway because sometimes we are not ready to receive the treasure. *The journey is more important than the destination. The process is just as vital as the result.*

The journey teaches us why the destination is important. And in our journey towards the destination we acquire the necessary virtues and character we need to possess before entering into the promised land. This is why patience is important. Because God is always teaching us something new and valuable everyday but if we are not patient and we want to receive the promises straightaway we will never be attentive or careful to discern the little things God is teaching us for our own good.

Joseph later learnt the virtue of patience. Although he was 17 when he received the vision of God's plan for his life he still had to wait 13 years until God manifested it in his life. In this time Joseph learnt many things, including patience. He learnt to be totally dependent upon God. He learnt how to trust and depend on Him during affliction and loneliness. He had opportunities to turn against God. We all do. He could have lost his patience, he could have lost his trust and his integrity, he could have reverted back to a life of sin. But he held unto hope.

Even when Potiphar's wife attempted to seduce him—day by day refusing to give up—he rejected all of her advances and in frustration cried out to her "how then can I do this great wickedness, and sin against God? [Gen 39:9]" We can be sure that there were times when Joseph was tempted, the odd occasion when he thought it might be good to succumb to her temptations. But Joseph was wise and patient. He trusted in God and understood that such a transgression would jeopardise the perfect plan God had ordained for his life. He therefore rejected her advances, he was faithful and awaited the perfect purpose and plan God had created him for.

Even when he was locked up for doing no wrong he still continued to wait patiently until God would choose the perfect time to fulfil the vision; and even in prison he continued to learn everyday.

Alas! the children of Israel did not hearken unto the lesson of patience which was showcased to them in the life of Joseph. For God did not keep them in the wilderness because he had pleasure in their affliction. But he kept them in the wilderness so that they could learn his ways—and inherit his holy character in the process—to later become the "kingdom of priests and holy nation [Exo 19:6]" he had chosen them to be.

It is written "all these things happened unto them for ensamples: and they were written for our admonition, upon whom the ends of the world are come [1 Cor 10:11]." God is therefore talking to us when we read the stories in the Old Testament. Just like God chose Israel to be a "kingdom of priests, and an holy nation" so too has he chosen us to be "a chosen generation, a royal priesthood, an holy nation, a peculiar people; that ye should shew forth the praises of him who hath called you out of darkness into his marvellous light [1 Pet 2:9]."

But many of the children of Israel did not receive the role and responsibility; for in their impatience and distrust they went a whoring after other idols, serving the gods of their own imagination. The men who were patient as Moses was called upon the mount were his brethren, many men who were of the tribe of Levi.

"Moses stood in the gate of the camp and said who is on the LORD's side? let him come unto me. And all the sons of Levi gathered themselves together unto him [Exo 32:26]."

God rewarded the Levites for their patience and their loyalty amidst the troubling and testing times by giving them the priesthood. So too will we become the holy priests of God—in a better priesthood of the order of Melchesidek—if we hold steadfast patient unto the end upon the coming of the Lord.

For the Lord, like Moses, will one day descend from a mount which is heavenly. The Lord, as he testifies in the parable of the goats and sheep, will separate those who are faithful from those who are not. Like he speaks of in the parable of the wise and foolish servants, there will be some who patiently await his second coming but there will also be others, evil and impatient servants, who "shall say in his heart, my Lord delayeth his coming; and shall begin to smite his fellowservants, and to eat and drink with the drunken [Matt 24:49]."

Is this not what the unfaithful children of Israel did as they rose up to drink, eat and play? Had they known Moses was to soon descend from the mount, had they known the wrath of God and the exact timing and seriousness of the punishment he was unexpectedly going to execute upon them, they would have surely abhorred the works of their hands and waited patiently for him to descend. For the Lord Jesus "shall come in a day when he [the servant] looketh not for him, and in an hour that he is not aware of, and shall cut him asunder, and appoint him his portion with the hypocrites: there shall be weeping and gnashing of teeth [Matt 24:50-51]."

Just like the impatient were cut off during the day Moses descended down from the mount in great indignation—whereby "there fell of the people that day about three thousand men [Exo 32:28]"—so too shall there be a great slaughter for those who in their impatience turn their back from the living God when he sends his Son to reign upon the earth. Jesus foreshadows these perilous days in his own words. "But those mine enemies, which would not that I should reign over them, bring hither, and slay them before me [Lk 19:27]."

Now these are words which we may not wish to hear but are they not written for our encouragement, written so that we might fear God and continue to hold steadfast in patience, even when our flesh cries out and our soul is languished in great confusion?

When the LORD descended upon mount Sinai in a great fire the children of Israel did not want to hear his words. "They said unto Moses speak thou with us, and we will hear: but let not God speak with us [Exo 20:19]." This is how many believers treat Jesus today, they say to their pastors speak thou to us, but we will not seek the Son of God ourselves.

God came down to prove the children of Israel, as Moses testified "that his fear may be before your faces, that ye sin not [Exo 20:20]." By coming down in a devastating show of strength and fire He was foreshadowing the dreadful fate they would inherit if they chose to disobey his commandments. The LORD is doing the same to us today— by the more peaceful means of his Son—for his words shall surely all be fulfilled.

A Way that Seems Right to Man

It is written "there is a way which seemeth right unto a man, but the end thereof are the ways of death [Pro 14:12]."

When we look at the downfalls of many people in the bible we see that this observation made by Solomon above is certainly true. Eve thought she made the right decision when she ate from the tree of the knowledge of good and evil. Sarah thought she made the correct decision when she told her maid Hagar to sleep with her husband Abram. The children of Israel thought they made an expedient choice when they fashioned the golden calf and created a sacrifice for their gods. And Saul in his impatience thought he made the right decision when he made a peace offering with burnt sacrifices without waiting for the prophet Samuel when he was expressly commanded to first wait for the prophet's return.

In this last example of impatience God teaches us a few significant lessons. Samuel told Saul to wait "seven days, according to the set time that Samuel had appointed." The king was to wait for the prophet's return then they would offer sacrifice to the LORD. But Samuel did not come at the time Saul had anticipated. So the king in his impatience disobeyed the commandment of the prophet and said "bring hither a burnt offering to me and peace offerings. And he offered the burnt offering [1 Sam 13:9]." He took matters into his own hands. But the moment "he had made an end of offering the burnt offering, behold, Samuel came [1 Sam 13:10]."

Samuel immediately rebuked the king. Because of his impatience and disobedience, he was told his kingdom would no longer last for ever and that he would later be replaced by a man better than him [1 Sam 13:13].

Jesus is teaching us many things from this episode. Firstly, Samuel gave Saul very specific instructions. So likewise, God will give us very specific instructions too. These instructions are found in the word of God. But if we are impatient, like Saul, then we will disobey these instructions and face penalties for doing so. We should be wise and continue to wait for all things, including his presence — for the moment we grow impatient and are tempted to disobey, is the very moment God is surely working to fulfil His promise for our own good. If Saul had waited just a little bit longer he would have seen Samuel coming as he had promised; but because he was impatient he was received with great disapproval.

If we disobey because of impatience we can lose our own hope of an eternal kingdom in much the same way Saul lost the opportunity to have his kingdom established forever.

Many religions have been constructed because of impatience. It takes diligence to seek the face of God. But because many are impatient they receive a religious substitute which requires less work. Now I am not saying we are saved by works alone. But when we have faith we must exercise appropriate works and one of these works is steadfast patience. Patience is good because it requires us to be dependent and reliant upon God. It is also good because it is a way of giving pure evidence for our faith in God. Jesus said "when the Son of man cometh, shall he find faith on the earth? [Lk 18:8]" This was because he could foresee the troubling times ahead of the saints which would require great patience on their part. Jesus prophesied that many false Christs and false prophets would arise. He said they would show great signs and wonders, that they would "say unto you, Behold, he is in the desert . . . behold, he is in the secret chambers [Matt 24:24,26]." These false prophets, who are religious by nature, will lead many people into places they should not be in. They will say Jesus Christ is here and there but he will not be. But because many people will be impatient—and "say in their heart, my Lord delayeth his coming [Matt 24:48]"—many will hearken unto their deception and worship the false golden calf which the book of Exodus foreshadows.

But Jesus Christ commands us to wait and watch. He exhorts us to be patient and to continue on in prayer. Jesus will eventually return and all will behold his descent; "for as the lightening cometh out of the east, and shineth even unto the west, so shall also the coming of the Son of man be [Matt 24:27]."

When we are patient we will learn to become more intimate with God. As we await certain promises in life we should focus on the one thing which is most important; becoming more close and intimate with God.

When we are patient we will also learn to reflect his character. For God himself is patient as the scripture also testify. "Be patient therefore, brethren, unto the coming of the Lord. Behold, the husbandman waiteth for the precious fruit of the earth, and hath long patience for it, until he receive the early and latter rain [Jas 5:7]."

God is patient towards us because he wants us to be conformed into the image of his Son and he wants us to become fruitful. This takes time but God understands this so he nourishes us in the meantime. God is patient so we must be patient. God is patient to us so we must be patient to others. Jesus as the embodiment of God was also patient. He was patient when the disciples continued to lack belief in him. And he was patient when they continued to ask questions which were simple and basic. Even when they betrayed him and fled from his face in the garden of Gethsamene, he was still patient and showed them his love, never retaliating after he was resurrected from the dead.

When we are patient we will make the best decisions in life. We will not be moved by emotion, by the opinions of others and of religion, but we will wait for God's perfect plan to materialise in our lives. Jesus had to wait all night before he chose the twelve disciples. He waited in prayer and did not leave until God gave him an answer. We too must have to wait—in all manner of significant decisions—before we make the right call ordained by God.

Appreciation

One of the most important lessons we can learn from our walk with God is appreciation. Appreciation is also known as gratitude. It is when we are thankful to God, for all that He has provided for us, no matter what situation or circumstance we might face in our life.

There are a number of examples of men and women, holy children of God, who were used mightily by God to execute supernatural works because of the unwavering root of gratitude which they possessed.

When God told Abraham that Sarah would conceive a newborn boy, the patriarch was already content with what the LORD had provided him. "Abraham said unto God, O that Ishmael might live before thee! [Gen 17:18]" Abraham did not covet more than what God had already provided him with but he was content in every circumstance he shared with God.

Paul told the Philippians "I have learned, in whatsoever state I am in, therewith to be content [Phi 4:11]." He made this statement whilst he was imprisoned for preaching the gospel.

And what about David? David was a man who certainly acquired the art of appreciation. In the 34th Psalm he says "I will bless the LORD at all times: his praise shall continually be in my mouth [Psa 34:1]." David wrote this psalm when he was escaping persecution from Saul. David in this psalm therefore exhorts the reader to bless and praise the LORD regardless of the situations life may confront us with. He understood that all situations have been ordained by a loving God: and that there must therefore be a good reason for us to endure difficult situations.

Although David had done no harm to king Saul, he still exhorted his audience to "bless the LORD at all times." This is because he understood the importance of gratitude. He also understood how "all things work together for good to them that love God, to them who are the called according to his purpose [Rom 8:28]." If we really believe this statement made by the holy Ghost and mediated by the Apostle Paul then we will certainly remain appreciative even when circumstances in life around us appear terrible.

Jesus Christ was the best example of a man who remained appreciative in his life. Despite the many terrible things which befell him he always gave thanks to God. Before he was tortured and crucified, "Jesus took bread, and blessed it, and brake it . . . and he took the cup, and gave thanks [Matt 26:26-27]." Jesus was aware that he would be betrayed shortly after. He knew that the scriptures had to be fulfilled and that he was about to face a great deal of suffering in the next few days. But Jesus still gave thanks to the LORD. After giving thanks to the Father, Jesus and his disciples sang a hymn. Jesus was grateful that God had given him the power and strength to overcome; and despite knowing the many things he was just about to suffer for our sake, "for the joy that was set before him [Heb 12:2]" he endured the great affliction which he undeservedly received, as he continued to give thanks to Him who was able to deliver him from the dead.

Murmuring

We can be sure that God wants us to remain appreciative and full of gratitude. One way which we can conclude that this is true is by reflecting on the travails which the Israelites suffered for their unappreciative and covetous attitude. When the children of Israel entered into the wilderness they continued to murmur and complain against the LORD.

"And when the people complained, it displeased the LORD: and the LORD heard it; and his anger was kindled and the fire of the LORD burnt among them, and consumed them that were in the uttermost parts of the camp [Num 11:1]."

The children of Israel were complaining because they remembered and longed for the benefits they received whilst they sojourned in Egypt. They did not complain once, twice or three times but they continued to complain and whine over and over again.

Now we know that this displeased God. And although the LORD had already punished some of them, "the children of Israel wept again, and said, who shall give us flesh to eat? [Num 11:4]" They were unhappy because they were stripped from the material comforts they once enjoyed in Egypt. Not knowing that this was only a temporary situation, a period of time which was necessary to purge them from the defilement they had possessed from the land of their captivity, they continued to complain about "the fish which we did eat in Egypt freely; the cucumbers, and the melons, and the leeks, and the onions and the garlick [Num 11:5]."

They could not forget the comforts they enjoyed in Egypt. God had provided them with food already, he provided them with manna which they used to bake bread. But the people were not content; they continued to weep and complain. "Then Moses heard the people weep through out their families, every man in the door of his tent: and the anger of the LORD was kindled greatly; Moses also was displeased [Num 11:10]."

This episode speaks volumes about God's disdain towards covetousness and complaining. God had provided His people with what they needed to survive. If they needed melons, garlick and fish then he would have surely provided it for them. But God was frustrated that they were so short-sighted and unthankful. He had done marvellous works for them, he had showed them great and miraculous signs. And above all he had just redeemed them from centuries of hard captivity: He had also promised them a change of circumstance, electing them as his chosen nation of royal priests. Nevertheless they continued to complain and the LORD heard it and was sorely displeased [Num 11:1].

This is how God feels when we complain against Him. Even if we murmur in our hearts He is not too pleased. There are two important reasons for this reaction from God. (1) When we murmur against God we reveal our covetous nature which God does not like. Covetousness is associated to greed and it reveals a strong desire for material possessions, often for another's possessions, at the expense of the possession of God's heart.

Covetousness is when a person craves a possession which he does not necessarily need. It is when he is unsatisfied for what God has already provided him. A great example of this is when David lusted after Bathsheeba after already having a number of wives. Covetousness and murmuring is connected because whenever we covet something we will naturally begin to murmur, beg and complain for what God has not provided us with, when what he has provided us with is already enough.

This is not pleasing to God because the LORD wants us to be satisfied with Him alone. He does not want us to place a greater deal of priority and longing towards objects which are destined to perish. But he wants us to focus and be satisfied by his presence and by his love alone. This is what he meant when he told Abraham, "I am thy shield, and thy exceeding great reward [Gen 15:1]." This is what David understood when he declared "one thing have I desired of the LORD, that will I seek after; that I may dwell in the house of the LORD all the days of my life, to behold the beauty of the LORD, and to enquire in his temple [Psa 27:4]."

This is what David communicates when he says "The LORD is my Shepherd; I shall not want [Psa 23:1]." David was saying that all I need is the LORD: and since I can always have the LORD at any moment of the day—even though I may lack all other things upon this earth—"I will [still] bless the LORD at all times [Psa 34:1]" for his presence will be sufficient. When we do not have this mindset then we are an offence to God. We will only want God when we desire a possession or a blessing from Him, we will operate like a goldigger and a mistress rather than a friend and a lover. This is something Moses understood too. There were many things the Prophet could have requested from the LORD, he was in a favourable position with God, but all he desired was His presence.

"And he said unto him, if thy presence go not with me, carry us not up hence [Exo 33:15]."

Moses was promised great wealth and possessions, he would have likely maintained his position of great authority upon arriving in the land of Canaan. This was a land brimming with milk and honey after all, but the man of God said all of it was nothing without the presence of God. It was seemingly impossible for Moses to express covetousness and ingratitude. For if God is your one and only desire, then you will always have peace because He is always near. "Am I a God who is only close at hand? says the LORD. No, I am far away at the same time [Jer 23:23]."

When we complain against God—particularly from a place of covetousness and ingratitude—then we reveal to Him that He alone is insufficient. God has given us all an open door: He said He will sup with us and commune with us if we let Him in [Rev 3:20]. But if we continue to complain against Him because He has not provided us with the possessions which we lust after, then we are ultimately saying to Him that He is insufficient. This is basically spiritual adultery.

If I had a wife and she did not satisfy me then I may commit adultery and find another wife. I would surely complain and reveal my ingratitude against her. And this is what we do—in spiritual terms—when we complain against God and seek out other things besides His presence alone. When the children of Israel fashioned a golden calf and served different foreign gods such as Baalim and Ashteroth it was a physical manifestation of an interior problem. The idolatry and adultery arose in their heart and eventually resulted in the worship of false gods. This is something which is dangerous for us to do because it is written that "thou shalt worship no other gods: for the LORD, whose name [is] jealous, [is] a jealous God [Exo 34:14]."

The greatest commandment is "thou shalt love the LORD thy God with all thy heart, and with all thy soul, and with all thy mind [Matt 22:37]." If we do this then we will neither covet not complain. As we have already shown, when we are covetous then we are likely to complain against God as did the Israelites. The flesh can never be satisfied. They longed for flesh and they were not satisfied with what God had provided them.

But if they loved God above all, if they loved him with all their heart and all of their soul, then they would have even eaten maggots if God had commanded them to do so. If they loved the LORD like Jesus did, then they would not have been concerned with any earthly gain but they would have said with sincere appreciation that "my meat is to do the will of him that sent me, and to finish his work [Jn 4:34]." When we desire nothing but the presence of God then we will always be satisfied. This is because Jesus said "lo, I am with you always, even unto the end of the world [Matt 28:20]." Jesus is always available.

Jesus' presence is joy and it is peace. If we seek him and abide in him then we will never be dissatisfied or discontent. God's presence is the source of all blessing. Which is why John in the book of Revelation says "Behold the tabernacle of God is with men and he will dwell with them . . . and shall wipe away all tears from their eyes, and there shall be no more death, neither sorrow, nor crying [Rev 21:3-4]." God's presence eradicates all woes. God wants the best for us. And He knows that He is the restorer of all of our woes. This is why it frustrates Him when we do not trust Him and seek Him.

When we complain against Him and seek those things which are only temporary at the expense of the peace of the Eternal God, then we do foolishly. We should not covet something in the world because God is greater than anything we could possibly covet. We should not complain because God is faithful to provide us with the very best solution and result at the best possible time.

(2) But another reason why the church may complain is because of

distrust. The children of Israel complained against God because they did not trust him and they felt he would not fulfil the promise he had made to take them into the promised land.

We too can complain against God when we fail to trust him. We can complain against God when we face undesirable circumstances in our lives, for example when we think he is doing a bad job or he is being too harsh and heavy upon us. This is what the children of Israel did on numerous occasions. They could not understand why they were going through so many ordeals to enter into the promised land. The journey should not have taken them so long. They soon lost faith and they returned back with their hearts into the idolatrous and profane customs they had inherited from Egypt. "And in their hearts turned back again into Egypt [Acts 7:39]."

This is a problem we might also face if we lose our ability to trust in God. When we decided to follow Jesus there were a number of things we had to abandon. We decided to live a holy life, completely free from sin, and we decided to live an exemplary life of righteousness. But because this path is narrow—it is difficult and requires us to daily crucify the flesh—there will certainly be some times when we question God, and when we earnestly ask ourselves whether what we are doing is of any value.

Even Jesus on the cross cried our "Father, Father, why have you forsaken me? [Matt 27:46]" So there will certainly be some instances in our lives when we might begin to lose trust and question the difficult life in Christ which we have chosen to embrace. This is what happened to the children of Israel. Although they were once ecstatic and hopeful when they had initially begun their journey and were redeemed from the clasp of Pharaoh, once they were confronted with a number of uncomfortable challenges and situations which appeared hopeless to overcome — they were now questioning and doubting whether God would take them into the land he had once promised them.

The children of Israel quickly lost faith in God. Because they no longer trusted in him they became totally unappreciative of all that he had done—all of the miracles and signs he had shown them and the tender-loving care he had shown them by liberating them from Egypt, were all quickly forgotten. Eventually, many of them were punished and were disqualified from entering into the promised land because of their rebellion. A reality which still speaks to us today:

"So we see that they could not enter in because of unbelief. Let us therefore fear, lest, a promise being left us of entering into his rest, any of you should seem to come short of it. For unto us was the gospel preached, as well as unto them: but the word preached did not profit them, not being mixed with faith in them that heard it [Heb 3:19-4:2]."

Remaining Thankful

One of the most important keys that we can possess in our daily walk with Christ is the ability to remain thankful. This is a secret which the Apostle Paul spoke of in a number of occasions. In his epistle to the Ephesians he exhorted the disciples to give "thanks always for all things unto God and the Father in the name of our Lord Jesus Christ [Eph 5:20]."

And in his first letter to the Thessalonians he exhorted them to "rejoice evermore [reminding them that] . . . in everything give thanks: for this is the will of God in Christ Jesus concerning you [1 Thes 5:16,18]." This last passage is very important for us because it clearly reveals that it is God's will for us to remain thankful in everything.

"In everything" means under every conceivable situation. In pain, "thank God," in loneliness "thank God," in peace, "thank God," in joy "thank God," in anxiety "thank God," in fear, "thank God," in persecution "thank God," in disappointment, "thank God." In whatsoever situation God places us in we must thank God with all of our hearts.

When we give thanks to God under every situation then He will certainly be pleased with us. This is a fact which is captured by the Apostle in the book of Hebrews. "By him therefore let us offer the sacrifice of praise to God continually, that is, the fruit of our lips giving thanks to his name . . . for with such sacrifices God is well pleased [Heb 13:15-16]."

The first question many of us may be tempted to ask—particularly during challenging and difficult situations—is why should I remain thankful? The most obvious and significant answer is: because of salvation. We should be thankful that God sent his only begotten Son to die on the cross for the forgiveness of our sins. We should be thankful that through his Son we are promised eternal life. We should be thankful that we are seated with Christ in heavenly places. We should be thankful that we have been chosen to be justified, sanctified and glorified forever more. The list really is endless.

But we must ask ourselves: do we really believe in the promises which have been outlined to us in the word of God? For if we do we should never complain. Jesus said that in this world we would face tribulation [Jn 16:33]. But Jesus never said we ought to complain or become unappreciative during these moments of great testing, but instead he told us to "be of good cheer; [reminding us] I have overcome the world [Jn 16:33]."

The big problem is that many of us believers are likely to be thankful and grateful during comfort and great blessing; but when the seasons change and we are greeted with unexpected conflict and great unease in this world many of us are then quick to complain and to become slumped in discontent. This is not the will of God. For he desires of us to be content and thankful under all circumstances we face in life. When we are going through difficult times in our lives we should be thankful too. The Apostle Paul said that "if we suffer we shall also reign with him [2 Tim 2:12]."

Jesus said we should "rejoice, and be exceeding glad" when we are persecuted and reviled for righteousness sake, "for great is your reward in heaven [Matt 5:12]." And this is exactly what the Apostles did when they were persecuted.

When the early Apostles were beaten and scourged for preaching Jesus they were exceedingly grateful that they had been given the opportunity by God to suffer in the name of Jesus. "And they departed from the presence of the council, rejoicing that they were counted worthy to suffer shame for his name [Acts 5:41]."

We hear of a similar story in the 16th chapter of the book of Acts when Paul and Silas were locked up in prison for again preaching the gospel. These men of God were thankful for life despite the ordeals they had to face and "at midnight Paul and Silas prayed, and sang praises unto God; and the prisoners heard them." After they were heard singing praises to God "there was a great earthquake, so that the foundations of the prison were shaken; and immediately all the doors were opened, and every one's bands were loosed [Acts 16:26]."

Many doors will be opened for us when we praise God and remain thankful. Paul and Silas were able to save and baptise a number of souls from those who were at hand to experience the mighty move of God. All of this occurred because the Apostles remained thankful. We too, therefore, will win souls at ease when we remain thankful during adversity — for many will marvel when they observe our joy and peace during the most hostile of circumstances, and many will surely be intrigued to hear about Jesus when we exhibit the great peace and security he provides us with.

Satan can only work through us, undermine us and control us, when he discerns that we are ungrateful. He was able to discern that Eve was unthankful in the Garden before he tempted her. He managed to work through Samson when he sent Delilah to him. He managed to work through David when the king saw Bathsehba bathing. All of these mistakes made by the people of God took place because they were living in a time of ungratefulness and covetousness.

One of the weapons the enemy can use to make us unthankful in Christ is by reminding us of the comfortable past we once used to live. He may remind us of the fornication, the alcohol, the old friends and drugs, the wealth and worldly popularity, the numerous pleasures of the flesh which once made our lives comfortable and content. If he can get us to remember the past then perhaps we will abandon God's calling for our lives and return to the world. Some Christians are discontent with God because the Christian walk is not the easiest and although God is there to support us with his holy Spirit there are certainly a number of sacrifices we must daily make in order to be at a right standing with Christ. Some of these sacrifices result in ingratitude and discontent. This is what happened in the life of Demas who forsook the Apostle Paul to return back to the world:

"For Demas hath forsaken me, having loved this present world, and is departed unto Thessalonica. [2 Tim 4:10]"

It is crucial for us to forget about the past and to look forward to the future, "when he [Jesus] shall have delivered up the kingdom to God, even the Father [1 Cor 15:24]." When I say "forget about the past," I do not mean that we should forget about the useful memories and lessons of the past, those of which have been useful in moulding us into the saint we are today, but what I am saying is that we ought to forget about those vain and profane actions, the many sins we once used to exercise on a daily basis in the past. Remember to ask yourself: "what fruit had ye then in those things whereof ye are now ashamed? for the end of those things is death [Rom 6:21]." And remember to continue to look forward: to await the impending coming of our Lord Jesus Christ and the great recompense he has in store for those who patiently and gratefully endure until he comes.

"Say not thou, what is the cause that the former days were better than these? for thou dost not enquire wisely concerning this [Ecc 7:10]."

Remember Lot's wife who was turned into a pillar of salt for looking back into Sodom and Gomorrah [Gen 19:26].

The children of Israel did this when they complained and longed after the good things they once enjoyed in Egypt. "We remember the fish, which we did eat in Egypt freely, the cucumbers, and the melons, and the leeks, and the onions, and the garlick [Num 11:5]." They did this a number of times. Another time, after they received a disheartening report from the spies sent into the land of Canaan, "they said one to another, let us make a captain, and let us return into Egypt [Num 14:4]." For their transgression—for their desire to return back to the life that God had just redeemed them from and their desire to discontinue the covenant God had just made with them—many were greatly punished. All of the congregation who were above the age of 20, save Joshua and Caleb, were forbidden from entering into the promised land.

Now the scripture says that we do "not enquire wisely concerning this," whenever we say "what is the cause that the former days were better than these [Ecc 7:10]." Life is experienced in cycles. Some days are comfortable and other days are anxious. Some days are joyful and others are sad. Life is always changing so we cannot expect our current situation to always be like the past. But when our life changes and it takes a tide for the worse then the common temptation is for us to subside into complaining and frustration towards God. This is what Solomon is saying when he says "say not thou, what is the cause that the former days were better than these?"

It is not wise for us to do this because (1) God does not like it when we lose faith and complain and (2) God is always teaching us particular lessons during every season. Nothing happens by chance, especially when we are under the guidance of God's Spirit, and difficult seasons are the best opportunities to bear more fruit to become like Christ. Indeed Paul commented upon this in his epistle to the Romans. "We glory in tribulations also: knowing that tribulation worketh patience; and patience, experience, and experience hope [Rom 5:3-4]."

God is sovereign. Therefore, God is in control during challenging times too. God is always teaching us something new everyday. Even during persecution and trials he is teaching us something new such as patience or humility.

God ultimately desires for us to be conformed into the image of His Son. He is daily teaching us to be like his only begotten Son. He wants us to be blameless, spotless and without blemish like His Son. Therefore, he will use persecution, trials and disappointments in life to purge us and perfect us. It is not wise to question the prior days of comfort because perhaps God is taking us through a turbulent time so that we can learn to depend upon Him more. We must remember and believe that "all things work together for good to them that love God, to them who are the called according to his purpose [Rom 8:28]."

When we go through difficult times and trials we must be still and focused and try to discern what God is teaching us during this particular time.

When Joseph was in the prison he could have complained and lost all hope. He did not deserve to be in prison but God placed him in there for a reason.

Joseph learnt many necessary skills whilst he stayed in the prison. These skills were helpful and necessary for the job he would later receive under Pharaoh. Joseph would later become a mighty leader, second in command under the king of Egypt. But he did not become a leader overnight. When he was sold into captivity by his brothers he found himself in Potiphar's house. Potiphar was the captain of the Egyptian army and God gave Joseph great favour in his household. Joseph was made the "overseer over his house," and such was his standing with his boss that he put "all that he had . . . into his [Joseph's] hand [Gen 39:4]."

We hear of the same story when Joseph was put into prison.

"And the keeper of the prison committed to Joseph's hand all the prisoners that were in the prison; and whatsoever they did there he was the doer of it [Gen 39:22]."

During trials and betrayals, God taught Joseph many invaluable lessons. God also used these seasons to mould Joseph's character and to develop within him an integral set of skills. Joseph could have been bitter but he always retained a strong sense of hope for his future. He was faithful that God would complete what He had begun; and he was faithful God would accomplish what He had promised to do for him in his life. We can only imagine that Joseph was thankful at all moments, even when he was being persecuted for doing no wrong. Otherwise he would not have stayed strong when Potiphar's wife tempted him or whilst he was imprisoned despite not being guilty for any wrongdoing.

We too will be challenged and tried by the world around us. We know this will happen in our lives because it is written "all who live godly in Christ Jesus shall suffer persecution [2 Tim 3:12]."

Sometimes God will even put us in difficult circumstances for our own good. This is what happened in the life of David before he became king. When David had killed Goliath he received great fame. And Saul, who was the king at this time, was understandably jealous. Because of Saul's rebellion against God he had lost favour. One day God sent an evil spirit upon Saul and the king sought to kill David with a javelin [1 Sam 19:9-10]. David managed to escape and flee into the wilderness. But it was God who was in control of Saul's actions because the scripture records how "the evil spirit from the LORD" was sent by Him to Saul.

God wanted David to flee into the wilderness because he wanted to teach him certain lessons. These lessons would serve him well when he later became king. David understood this and he kept focused on the vision which God had laid upon his heart. He knew, and believed, he would one day become the king so he refused to complain about the process and he remained resilient and thankful during the temporary battles he had to fight in the wilderness.

God has promised us many extraordinary things too. If we remain focused on these good things, and these extraordinary promises, then we will never be unthankful. But we will thank God for the trials which enable us to excel even more. The Apostles thanked God for the opportunity to suffer for Jesus. Shall we not also remain thankful during adversity?

"Every branch in me that beareth not fruit he taketh away: and every branch that beareth fruit, he purgeth it, that it may bring forth more fruit [Jn 15:2]."

The Apostle Paul exhorted Timothy to look upon the things which are unseen as opposed to the things which are seen. "For the things which are seen are temporary but the things which are unseen are eternal [2 Cor 4:18]." Many of the things which God has promised us are unseen. Nevertheless, they are also eternal.

The suffering we go through is only temporary whilst the promises we receive by remaining steadfast in Jesus' name are eternal and of unimaginable value. Is this not a cause to give thanks?

Paul says "for our light affliction which works a much more exceeding and eternal weight of glory [2 Cor 4:17]." He says in another epistle "that I do not think our current sufferings are worthy to be compared to the glory which shall be revealed in us [Rom 8:18]." When Paul exhorted the Thessalonians to "rejoice evermore [1 Thess 5:16]" he was in prison. But because of Paul's possession of Christ— his friendship with the Lord and his inheritance of eternal life too—he was able to remain sincerely thankful during some of the most bitter trials. We should remain thankful because we have received Christ. He who possesses Christ has possessed all things.

Intimacy with God is The Most Important

The first step we can take before we become intimate with God is the most important. This step is called faith. This is because we cannot approach God—talk to him, commune with him and follow him—unless we actually have faith in him. Ask yourself: is it possible to follow someone who is not real? Abraham is called the father of the faith. He is also called a friend of God. He became a friend of God because he believed in Him. We cannot become intimate with somebody we do not believe in. "For he that cometh to God must believe that he is, and that he is a rewarder of them that dilligently seek him [Heb 11:6]." So the first and most important step is faith.

There is only one key thing we must believe in before we step into greater intimacy with God. This belief must be retained in our minds and in our hearts for the remainder of our lives. This is the belief of Jesus Christ. That Jesus Christ, the Son of God, was delivered on the cross for the forgiveness of our sins, and raised up from the dead on the third day for our justification, only to then ascend into heaven to be seated at the right hand of the Father. He is working to establish God's kingdom upon the earth and we will reign and rule with him if we turn away from our sins and follow him daily. This is called the gospel. And without the gospel we cannot see, hear, touch, smell or taste of God: " for there is one God, and one mediator between God and men, the man Christ Jesus [1 Tim 2:5]."

Jesus Christ is the middle man between man and God. If we do not believe in Jesus then we do not believe in God. God was inside of Jesus so if we do not believe in Jesus then we do not believe in God. And if we do not believe on Him who was inside of Jesus then how can we become intimate with Him? Jesus said "he that believeth on me: believeth not on me, but on him who sent me [Jn 12:44]." And again: "believest thou not that I am in the Father, and the Father in me? the words that I speak unto you I speak not of myself: but the Father that dwelleth in me, he doeth the works [Jn 14:10]." "He that loveth me not keepeth not my sayings: and the word which ye hear is not mine, but the Father's which sent me [Jn 14:24]."

When I believed in Jesus Christ, in the claims made about his life and the hope of the gospel, I received the Holy Ghost. This is how I knew without a shadow of doubt that Jesus Christ is the Lord and that he is still alive today reigning from heaven. Because John the Baptist said "I indeed baptize you with water unto repentance: but he that cometh after me is mightier than I, whose shoes I am not worthy to bear: he shall baptise you with the Holy Ghost, and with fire [Matt 3:11]."

The Holy Ghost is the breathe of God. Before we receive the holy Spirit we must repent and believe in the Son of God [Acts 2:38]. Jesus said "he that believeth on me . . . out of his belly shall flow rivers of living water . . . this spake he of the Spirit [Jn 7:38-39]." And in another place it is written, "when the Comforter is come, whom I will send unto you from the Father, even the Spirit of truth, which proceedeth from the Father, he shall testify of me [Jn 15:26]."

We can only receive the gift of the Holy Spirit when we believe in Jesus Christ: in his death, resurrection and his ascension. This is important because we can only know God when we have the holy Spirit abiding within us.

"For what man knoweth the things of a man, save the spirit of man which is in him? even so the things of God knoweth no man, but the Spirit of God [1 Cor 2:11]."

The Holy Spirit teaches us about the nature of God. It is the Holy Spirit which draws us into the presence of God and stirs us to maintain fellowship with Him. Jesus said "he shall teach you all things, and bring all things to your remembrance, whatsoever I have said unto you [Jn 14:26]." The Holy Ghost is Jesus Christ inside of us, the hope of glory. Jesus Christ was extraordinarily close to God. He maintained that "I and my Father are one [Jn 10:30]." So if Jesus Christ lives inside of us then we will naturally draw closer to the Father.

Jesus said "except a man be born again he cannot see the kingdom of God [Jn 3:3]." In other words except a man be born again of the Spirit of God he cannot see the Father. We may ask ourselves if we cannot see the Father how can we have a relationship with him?

Jesus Christ said in another place "blessed are the pure in heart: for they shall see God [Matt 5:8]." The bible says that our hearts are wicked and deceitful above all things [Jer 17:9]. But when we receive the Spirit of God then our hearts begin the process of becoming purified. Jeremiah prophesied of this time when he spoke of the New Covenant: "I will put my law in their inward parts, and write in their hearts; and will be their God, and they shall be my people [Jer 31:33]." Ezekiel prophesied of this too when God told him "I will put a new spirit within you; and I will take the stony heart out of their flesh, and will give them a heart of flesh [Eze 11:19]." God fulfilled these prophecies through Jesus Christ. And we became the recipients of these great promises when we placed our faith in his name.

God gave us a new heart when we called on the name of his Son. He also gave us a new Spirit. It is this grace, which we have received through faith, which gave us the gift of daily fellowship with the Father. As it is written "as many as received him, to them gave he power to become the sons of God, even to them that believe on his name [Jn 1:12]."

We are the sons of God because we have received the Spirit of God. God decided to call Jesus his Son because he had a relationship with Him. Jesus was not only a servant but also a Son. A servant does not have a close relationship with the Master but a Son has a great and intimate relationship with his Father. A Son is a friend of the Father and he knows many of the secrets which are not necessarily disclosed to the servant.

Jesus Christ has called us to be sons of God whilst God has called us to be his friends. "Henceforth I call you not servants; for the servant knoweth not what his lord doeth: but I have called you friends; for all things that I have heard of my Father I have made known unto you [Jn 15:15]." Friends love to spend time with one another. They disclose their problems to one another and they have a perfect trust with one another, a perfect understanding of each others ways.

Jesus Christ has called us a friend and God has called us a Son.

God sent Jesus Christ into this world "to redeem those that were under the law, that we might receive the adoption of Sons [Gal 4:5]." God sent Jesus Christ into the world, delivered him onto a cross and raised him from the dead, so that we might receive the Spirit of his Son in our hearts, crying, Abba, Father [Gal 6:4]. Jesus Christ is the source of all intimacy with God. Believing in Jesus Christ is not sufficient but we must also have Jesus Christ living inside of us to be intimate with God. Jesus Christ said "without me ye can do nothing [Jn 15:5]." This is true: because we cannot receive the Holy Ghost unless we rely upon Jesus. We cannot even understand scripture—which helps us to become closer to God—unless we first learn to rely upon the grace of Christ.

After Jesus Christ had risen from the dead he drew near to his disciples "but their eyes were holden that they should not know him [Lk 24:16]." They were lamenting his death and missing his presence. Although some of the woman had told them that they had seen visions of angels who had told them to report back to them about his resurrection, "their words seems to them as idle tales, and they believed them not [Lk 24:11]."

When Jesus appeared to his disciples they did not recognise him at first. But after he later revealed his identity to them, "he expounded unto them in all the scriptures the things concerning himself [Lk 24:27]." This was not the first time Jesus had done this. But this time "their eyes were opened, and they knew him; and he vanished out of their sight [Lk 24:31]."

The disciples were awestruck. "And they said one to another, did not our heart burn within us, while he talked with us by the way; and while he opened to us the scriptures? [Lk 24:32]." The disciples could not understand the scriptures. Nobody could unless they had received the unction from God. The Pharisees knew the scriptures inside out but they still failed to acknowledge the words of God which proceeded from the mouth of the Messiah. But we hear of how Jesus gave his disciples the unction.

"Then opened he their understanding, that they might understand the scriptures [Lk 24:45]."

This is not the only illustration the Bible gives us about Jesus' grace. When Jesus met Peter at the lake of Gennesaret the disciple was in his ship. Jesus told him to thrust his net into the lake but Peter objected saying "master, we have toiled all the night, and have taken nothing [Lk 5:5]." However, Peter eventually hearkened unto Jesus' request.

"And when they had this done, they inclosed a great multitude of fishes: and their net brake [Lk 5:6]."

The same story happened again after Jesus had resurrected from the dead. Peter had returned to his profession as a fisherman. He was joined by some of the disciples at the sea of Tiberius, "and that night they caught nothing [Jn 21:3]." But when Jesus appeared everything changed. Jesus told them to cast the net on the right side of the ship. When Peter obliged and cast the net into the sea the net was full of great fishes, 153 of them, "yet was not the net broken [Jn 21:11]."

Jesus Christ was teaching his disciples what he had told them already: "without me ye can do nothing [Jn 15:5]." They could not cast out demons, heal the sick, catch fishes and win souls, unless they relied upon Jesus. Neither can we become intimate with the Father unless we rely upon Jesus.

Trusting in God/Reliance in Christ

Reliance upon Jesus is key. To rely means to trust and depend upon him. Unless we rely upon Jesus we cannot receive fellowship with God. This is something the Apostle John understood. In the gospel of John we hear of how the Apostle leaned on Jesus' breast at supper [Jn 21:20]. John under the inspiration of the Holy Ghost, wrote this down to communicate a spiritual truth to us. When he was leaning on Jesus Christ he was communicating the need for the disciples to lean upon the chest of Jesus. To lean means to rely upon something or somebody. If I lean upon a wall or a chair I am relying upon it to support me. So if I lean upon the chest of Jesus, as did John, I am learning to rely upon the Lord to support me in all my endeavours.

John leaned upon Jesus' chest during supper. They were eating together and we too can eat with Jesus whilst we are here upon this earth. The food which we eat is spiritual: it is the bread from heaven which is the word of God. This is why Jesus invites us to sup with him; he stands at the door knocking and says "if any man hear my voice, and open the door, I will come into him and will sup with him and he with me [Rev 3:20]."

When John was leaning upon the chest of Christ during supper he was communicating one key thing: lean upon the word of God. Rely upon the word of Jesus Christ. Unless we learn to lean upon the promises of Christ, we will find it difficult to sustain a relationship with God. This is because when persecution and temptations arise they can prevent us from continuing our walk to follow God. But if we decide to rely upon the words of Christ and do them during all circumstances, when the rain descends, the wind blows and the floods come, the house will certainly not fall, "for it is founded upon a rock [Matt 7:24-25]."

We must therefore learn to lean upon the chest of Jesus Christ. We must learn to "trust in the LORD with all thine heart; and lean not unto thine own understanding [Pro 3:5]."

The presence of God abides upon people who trust in him. The presence of God is something we must walk and turn towards before we can first experience it regularly. This is why it is written in the book of Zechariah "turn ye unto me, saith the LORD of hosts, and I will turn unto you [Zec 1:3]." And in the epistle of James: "draw nigh to God, and he will draw nigh to you [Jas 4:8]."

If we do not trust in God then we will certainly not choose to draw near to him. But if we do and we love him as well, then we will certainly feel compelled to draw nigh to God all the time.

We do this by obeying his commandments, by praying and speaking to him like a friend, in worship and in fasting, and also by reading his word.

If we trust in God then we will follow God. And if we follow God then we will trust in Jesus. And if we trust in Jesus then Jesus will follow us. This is why it is written that John was "the disciple whom Jesus loved following [Jn 21:20]." Jesus loved following John because John loved leaning on his breast. If we lean on Jesus—that is to say trust in him and his word—then the presence of Christ will also love to follow us around as he did with John.

Why Should I Trust in God? The Gospel

I have met a number of people who doubt their salvation. One friend in particular asked: "how do I know that I am saved?" I replied that I knew because of faith. The bible says that we are saved by grace through faith; "and that not of yourselves: it is the gift of God: not of works, lest any man should boast [Eph 2:8-9]."

Salvation is a gift from God through faith and not something we can earn in return. The only way we can earn salvation is by sincerely believing that Christ Jesus is Lord.

"That if thou shalt confess with thy mouth the lord Jesus. and shalt believe in thine heart that God hath raised him from the dead, thou shalt be saved [Rom 10:9]."

When we believe we will receive the gift of salvation from God. Faith is the root of receiving all gifts from God. Through our faith in Jesus we are given the gift of the Holy Ghost, which is the operational grace in our life which enables us to do the good works which are alluded to in the book of James [Jas 2:26]. They are not our works but the works of the Holy Spirit which is inside of us. "For it is God which worketh in you both to will and to do of his good pleasure [Phi 2:13]." So it is not our works which save us; but it is the work of faith, which gives us grace, which saves us from the world. "Therefore it is of faith, that it might be by grace, to the end the promise might be sure to all the seed; not to that only which is of the law, but to that also which is of the faith of Abraham; who is the father of us all [Rom 4:16]."

Many people doubt their salvation because they do not quite understand the nature of grace. If they understood that salvation was a free gift from God found in the death and resurrection of Jesus Christ then they would not be so anxious and fearful, ever working tirelessly to and fro as if salvation was something we ought to labour to receive. We must certainly obey Jesus if we want to enter into the kingdom of God. But if we do not obey Jesus and we say that we believe in him then this faith is certainly questionable.

If we believe in Jesus then we will be like Jesus. But if we say we believe in Jesus and do not obey Jesus then this faith is certainly counterfeit. If we believe only part of Jesus' commandments and chose to obey only a few of them then yes we may believe in Jesus but this is surely another Jesus—not the real Jesus—who is represented in the gospel of the Apostles. But if we really believe in Jesus Christ, the real Messiah who is written of in the New Testament, then we will surely do his works. "He that saith he abideth in him ought himself also to walk, even as he walked [Jn 2:6]."

It is grace, through the Holy Ghost, which enables us to do his works. These are the works of obedience which James talks about in his epistle. They are not carnal works and ordinances which bring us salvation but works which flow naturally from the rivers of living water which is the Holy Ghost inside us all.

The Apostle James—when he made the famous assertion that "faith without works is dead [Jas 2:26]"—was addressing counterfeit believers in the church who believed they could simply believe in Christ and continue to live on in sin. We know this to be true because he addresses and highlights this problem when he says "whosoever shall keep the whole law, and yet offend in one point he is guilty of all [Jam 2:10]." James was concerned with members of the church who said they believed in Christ but did not obey him. He was highlighting how such believers are counterfeit and unreal. For real faith will produce works, fruits of obedience and righteousness. And even as Abraham obeyed God in deciding to sacrifice his son Isaac, so too will real believers in Christ who will decide to sacrifice all to follow God.

"He that saith I know him and keepeth not his commandments is a liar and the truth is not in him [1 Jn 2:4]."

We should trust God for our salvation, not because we are any special or because we deserve any merit for our own works, but because He is faithful in what he has done by sending his Son to die for us on the cross.

Paul understood this point and elaborated it in many of his epistles. In the book of Romans for example he said "if Abraham were justified by works, he hath whereof to glory, but not before God [Rom 4:2]." Abraham was not justified for his works alone but he was justified by his faith in God. This faith gave him the grace to do good works.

The same applies to us today. Abraham believed God and it was imputed unto him for righteousness. In other words Abraham believed God and for this reason alone God gave him the gift of His own righteousness. "Now it was not written for his sake alone, that it was imputed to him; But for us also, to whom it shall be imputed, if we believe on him that raised up Jesus our Lord from the dead; who was delivered for our offence, and raised again for our justification [Rom 4:23-25]."

But what about faith without works? The works which God required in us, before he imputed his righteousness into us, was mainly obedience. For example God told Abraham to leave the land of Ur and to go to Canaan. This was a work of obedience which later resulted in his salvation. God will tell us similar things before he gives us his holy Ghost. For example we will be told to repent, stop fornicating, "he that steal let him steal not more [Eph 4:28] Etc. "

Right before Jesus Christ died on the cross "he said it is finished: and he bowed his head, and gave up the ghost [Jn 19:30]." Jesus Christ was declaring that the work of salvation—for the remission of our sins—was finished the very moment he died for us upon the cross. All we must do is believe that this is true. For our salvation is a gift from God.

We must trust in this promise and continue to walk in obedience. For the promise is a New Covenant, and any covenant is binding between two parties with certain obligations and promises which come as a result. The obligations of the covenant are outlined in a famous segment found within the book of Romans. We must (1) confess with our mouths that Jesus is Lord and (2) believe with all of our heart that God has raised him from the dead. (3) If we do this we will live according to God's will for us in this life, "for with the heart man believeth unto righteousness, and with the mouth confession is made unto salvation [Rom 10:10]." If we comply with these obligations then we will surely receive the promises of the New Covenant. God cannot lie so let us trust in him and believe in his promises. For we cannot please him unless we trust in him.

Life will not always be easy. "We must through much tribulation enter into the kingdom of God [Acts 14:22]." But God has promised to never leave nor forsake us. And he has told us that all things work together for our good.

The Apostle Paul is a man who through many experiences, great ordeals and oppositions, learnt to place all trust in God. He recalls to Timothy how "at my first answer no man stood with me, but all men forsook me . . . notwithstanding the Lord stood with me, and strengthened me [2 Tim 4:17]." He testifies how "I was delivered out of the mouth of the lion [Ibid]," and boldly proclaims "the Lord shall deliver me from every evil work, and will preserve me unto his heavenly kingdom [2 Tim 4:18]." These are the words of a man who clearly trusted in God. Despite his many struggles he understood and possessed a great deal of faith in God. This enabled him to endure all types of odds.

We possess this type of faith if want to receive the keys to eternal life.

Meschach, Shadrach and Abednego were delivered from a fiery furnace because they trusted in God. Even Nebuchadnezzar who had initially sought to punish them testified of their trust when he said "blessed be the God of Shadrach, Meschach, and Abednego, who hath sent his angel, and delivered his servants that trusted in him [Dan 3:28]."

The same thing happened to Daniel when he was delivered into a lion's den. "Daniel was taken up out of the den, and no manner of hurt was found upon him, because he believed in his God [Dan 6:23]." All of these men were delivered from death because they trusted in God. They were given the gift of prolonging their lives and evading death because they trusted in God. They were not delivered from their persecutions because of their works but because they trusted in God. The same applies to us today. We are delivered from all of the calamities which are the thrown at us in this life when we simply trust in Jesus Christ. We are able to evade the terrible consequences of sin when we trust in God. We are able to overcome all forms of sin by trusting in Him. Not because of our works but by the free gift of God which we receive when we simply trust him.

"There remaineth therefore a rest to the people of God. For he that is entered into his rest, he also hath ceased from his own works, as God did from his. Let us labour therefore to enter into that rest, lest any man fall after the same example of unbelief. [Heb 4:9-11]"

We should learn to trust in God because of his nature. God is love. God is the source of all power and authority. God is all sovereign, he owns all things and has the power to change all things whenever he likes. If we believe this to be true: then why won't we trust in him? If God is all-loving: then we should trust and know that all situations which we face in this life—whether they appear good or bad—are certainly for our own good. And if we believe God to be all-powerful then we will surely trust in him to deliver us from all calamity.

Especially when we are living righteously in accordance to his word. " For . . . no good thing will he withhold from them that walk uprightly [Psa 84:11]." If we do not trust in God then we reveal to him our unbelief in his declared nature.

When God told Abraham that his wife Sarah would bear him a son, "Sarah laughed within herself." She did not believe in the promise of God because she was old. She no longer had her monthly period [Gen 18:12]. She did not really believe that "with God nothing is impossible." Therefore she could not trust him.

"And the Lord said unto Abraham, Wherefore did Sarah laugh, saying, Shall I of a surety bear a child, which am old?" [Gen 18:13]

God can discern whenever we fail to trust him. The thoughts of our heart are laid open to him who sees and knows all things. And whilst we may pretend to others, we can never pretend before God. "God knows those who are his [2 Tim 2:19]." God knows those who trust in him and those who do not. He knows those who sincerely believe in his Son and those who only make believe.

"If we believe not, yet he abideth faithful: he cannot deny himself [2 Tim 2:13]." God's eternal character is independent from our faith in him. And even if everybody in the world denied the fact that God existed this would still not change the fact that God does indeed exist. For every 100 people who do not trust in God there are still at least another person who will place all their trust in him.

Cain did not trust in God but Abel did. Esau did not trust in God but Jacob did. Saul did not trust in God but David did. Judas failed to trust in God whilst Peter did trust in Christ. "Blessed are all they that put their trust in him [Psa 2:12]." The men who have trusted in God have become the recipients and benefactors of his inexhaustible grace. They "subdued kingdoms, wrought righteousness, obtained promises, stopped the mouths of lions, quenched the violence of fire, escaped the edge of the sword, out of weakness were made strong, waxed valiant in fight, turned to fight the armies of the aliens [Heb 11:33-34]." They accomplished all of these great feats because they simply placed their trust in God.

If any man does not trust God, "let not that man think that he shall receive anything of the Lord. A double-minded man is unstable in all his ways [Jas 1:7-8]." God reserves his promises and great spiritual treasures for those who learn to place all their trust in him. These are they who trust in God at all times. Not only when life is comfortable and the air sweet, but also when life is difficult and the circumstances unbearable.

"Trust in him at all times" says David [Psa 62:8]. God never changes. His character of love, mercy, power and patience does not diminish or disappear so neither must our trust in him, even when we go through circumstances we cannot quite understand. A double-minded man can only trust in God when his life appears favourable on the surface. But the moment temptation or persecution compasses him he will certainly run back into the world and forget his covenant which he has made with God.

The man who trusts in God at all times "shall be as a tree planted by the waters . . . and that spreadeth out her roots by the river, and shall not see when it cometh, but her leaf shall be green, and shall not be careful in the year of drought, neither shall cease from yielding fruit [Jer 17:8]." Those who trust in God will be surrounded by his presence at all times. They will be patient and wise. When the 'heat' of persecution and the 'drought' of reviling arise they will hold steadfast and their root will not be moved. They shall never cease from yielding the fruit of the Spirit and they shall prosper in everything God achieves through them.

God will not scold us if we have not trusted him in the past. We need not lament on our prior displays of unbelief. We must simply learn to trust him today. Not only today but for the remainder of our lives. God may not have been pleased with Sarah when she laughed in her heart through disbelief, but the matriarch evidently changed her life and later learnt the necessity of trusting in God. For in the book of Hebrews we are told "through faith also Sara herself received strength to conceive seed and was delivered of a child when she was past age, because she judged him faithful who had promised [Heb 11:11]."

We too should learn to trust God so that we might become more available to receive from his vast reservoir of grace. Undoubtedly times will arise when our faith is put into question. If this were not the case, then life would not be called the "good fight of faith [1 Tim 6:12]."

Life is certainly an ongoing test of faith. But whenever we are put to the test in this life, we must recall the words of God which were spoken to Abraham and Sarah: "is anything too hard for the LORD? [Gen 18:14]."

Whenever we do grow weary in faith, whenever the circumstances of life assault us and attempt to erode our trust in him, let us meditate on the omnipotent nature of our wonderful God. "Ah Lord God! behold, thou hast made the heaven and the earth by thy great power and stretched out arm, and there is nothing too hard for thee [Jer 32:17]." This will strengthen us and invigorate us in time of need.

We need to become intimate with him so we that can trust him. We only trust people who we know. So we must grow in our experiential knowledge of God so that we might learn to trust him more. Victory breeds confidence. And experiences bring about greater clarity. When we experience more of God we are more aware of his nature. And the more we know about the nature of God the more we will come to trust him.

Rest: The Presence

One of the most notable indications of God's presence upon us is rest. God said to Moses, "my presence shall go with thee, and I will give thee rest [Exo 33:14]."

This rest denotes a lack of activity and labour. The rest God speaks about is spiritual rather than physical. When we rest in the physical we are at peace. We do not desire anything besides the peace our rest provides us with and we are totally content in it. When we are resting we are often leaning upon something. Some rest upon a chair, some upon a wall and others upon a bed. To rest denotes to cease upon striving, to cease upon labouring.

When I am tired and I have returned from an exhausting day of work I may even lose my appetite to cook before I sleep. I will certainly not harbour the desire to go to the gym, and although I may have wanted to watch an important broadcast on the television earlier on in the day, now that I desire rest, all other things will become secondary. All desires which I initially had during the day will now subside because I require rest. And now this rest will be the selected source of peace and satisfaction.

The peace I receive during this rest is so great that my initial yearnings for other things—which were found outside of this rest—are now forgotten and pushed aside.

This is how we understand the rest which is provided to us by the presence of God. The same which is noted by this physical rest can also be provided to us by God when we receive his spiritual rest.

"And he said, my presence shall go with thee, and I will give thee rest [Exo 33:14]."

When we experience the presence of God we receive peace. Peace is a feeling we receive during satisfaction and our satisfaction is derived from our success to achieve certain targets. For instance, if I wanted to win a certain competition, winning it will give me peace. If I want a wife, and I am desperate to find one, I will only receive peace when I finally get her. If I am struggling with a health concern. and it refuses to leave me, I will be robbed of my peace so long it continues to bother me.

But when we receive the presence of God, and the accompaniment of his peace, all of these concerns will evaporate immediately. This is the rest which God spoke to Moses when he told him "I will give thee rest." A rest which results in being content and satisfied in God's presence alone. Only then, when we experience this, can we be certain of God's presence. Only then, when all concerns, agendas, ambitions and anxieties are gone, can we be sure that the thick presence of God's Spirit has surely invaded our atmosphere.

This is the rest only Jesus Christ can provide. A peace which is independent from any of the circumstances which are found in the observable world. A peace which will make you immune to anything which the devil may place in front of you. A rest which will enable you to be satisfied and joyful at all times.

Jesus Christ invited all to receive this rest.

"Come unto me, all ye that labour and are heavy laden, and I will give you rest [Matt 11:28]."

The rest which was promised to Moses is the rest which all of us can receive through Jesus Christ. This rest is better than the rest which is found in the world because it is not contingent upon the changing nature of the temporal and natural world. If your source of rest is found in man then this rest will only be limited. Friends will let you down, families will do so too; so through them there can be found no real rest therein. And if your rest is found in money which can plummet in value at any moment of time, then neither can this rest be maintained.

Rest cannot be found in the world because it is in constant movement. Relationships are ever being formed and broken; money is being made and lost; people are being born and others are dying; the sun is always rising then setting; it is clear that God has fashioned this natural world in such a way that rest cannot be found therein.

The opposite of rest is activity. And I dare you to be bold and look around you: is not everything in activity? Even the stones which are inanimate are disposed to erode. The sun is destined to one day disappear. And everything you see before you will one day go. "Heaven and earth shall pass away, but my words shall not pass away [Matt 24:35]."

This is why man cannot find rest upon this earth unless it be through Him. This is why the flesh cannot provide us peace. How can something which will one day go give me peace? How can I rest upon something which will one day be broken? If I were to marry today, with the knowledge my wife would die in six months, would my consummation with her provide me any peace? Or what if I had a son and I knew he would be taken away from me in a couple of months, would I find rest from this fact? The only things which can provide man with rest and peace are spiritual things. "For to be carnally minded is death; but to be spiritually minded is life and peace [Rom 8:6]." The only things in which we can assuredly rest upon are eternal things. All other things are like shadows which are accompanied with illusions of rest and peace.

The rest which Jesus Christ offers us is different. It is eternal and cannot be taken away from us. This is the rest which Mary of Bethany received. Jesus Christ attested of this fact when he told Martha, "one thing is needful: and Mary hath chosen that good part, which shall not be taken away from her [Lk 10:42]."

Martha, on the other hand, was careful and troubled about many things [Lk 10:41]. Although she served the Lord and knew him well, she still found no peace. "Martha was cumbered about much serving and came to him [Lk 10:40]." Serving the Lord does not necessarily result in rest. Our ministries which we have in the name of Jesus, no matter how successful they may be, will not provide us with the peace and rest we all desire.

Only Jesus Christ can give us this. For our ministries and our service will one day go; the popularity, the support and authority will also one day go. But for the bride of Jesus Christ, who craves the presence of God, Jesus is that one "good part, which shall not be taken away from her [Lk 10:42]."

The things which are temporal belong to the world. Whereas the treasures which are eternal belong to God. It is therefore vain to chase shadows and to collect dust and copper which rust, when we cannot take these things with us into the realm in which we will reside in forever. This is the understanding which Solomon received when he was led to conclude by God that all is vanity.

But he did not stop their because he also exhorted the audience to "fear God, and [to] keep his commandments [Ecc 12:13]." If we fear God and keep his commandments then we will not live a vain life. For God will reward the obedient soul with riches which cannot be lost. "Treasures in heaven, where neither moth nor rust doth corrupt, and where thieves do no break through nor steal [Matt 6:20]." These are the treasures of knowledge and wisdom. Treasures which are hidden in Jesus Christ [Col 2:3].

Jesus Christ was never concerned about the acquisition of temporal riches. His riches were from above in the bosom of the Father. If we are in Christ we must follow suit. We must receive a rest from above and not from below.

"If ye then be risen with Christ, seek those things which are above, where Christ sitteth on the right hand of God. Set your affection on things above, not on things on the earth [Col 3:1-2]."

According to John, the things of "the world passeth away", whereas the things which belong to God abide for ever [1 Jn 2:16]. This means that the rest of this world will pass away, whereas the rest which belongs to God, will remain for ever. James says that Father of lights has "no variableness, neither shadow of turning [Jas 1:17]." If we receive God's nature—which is eternal and immutable—then we will also receive his gifts and riches which are also without variableness and shadow of turning.

Let us therefore receive the rest of God which does not change, diminish or suddenly disappear.

David understood this and was led to assess how "God is a refuge for us [Psa 62:8]." In another psalm he writes "He is my refuge and my fortress: my God, in him will I trust [Psa 91:2]." A refuge is a place where anybody can rest. God is an eternal refuge. He is a Spirit who can provide all spirits with the rest all beings assuredly desire. He is the only refuge who can give man the rest that he requires. When he receives the rest of the Father he will be content and satisfied. He shall have no want. Remember the words of David who I believe attained unto this rest:

"The LORD is my shepherd; I shall not want [Psa 23:1]"

Printed in the United States
By Bookmasters